Harvard
Business
Review

ON

WOMEN IN BUSINESS

THE HARVARD BUSINESS REVIEW PAPERBACK SERIES

The series is designed to bring today's managers and professionals the fundamental information they need to stay competitive in a fast-moving world. From the preeminent thinkers whose work has defined an entire field to the rising stars who will redefine the way we think about business, here are the leading minds and landmark ideas that have established the *Harvard Business Review* as required reading for ambitious businesspeople in organizations around the globe.

Other books in the series:

Harvard Business Review Interviews with CEOs

Harvard Business Review on Advances in Strategy

Harvard Business Review on Appraising Employee Performance

Harvard Business Review on Becoming a High Performance Manager

Harvard Business Review on Brand Management

Harvard Business Review on Breakthrough Leadership

Harvard Business Review on Breakthrough Thinking

Harvard Business Review on Building Personal and Organizational Resilience

Harvard Business Review on Business and the Environment

Harvard Business Review on the Business Value of IT

Harvard Business Review on Change

Harvard Business Review on Compensation

Harvard Business Review on Corporate Ethics

Harvard Business Review on Corporate Governance

Harvard Business Review on Corporate Responsibility

Harvard Business Review on Corporate Strategy

Harvard Business Review on Crisis Management

Harvard Business Review on Culture and Change

Harvard Business Review on Customer Relationship Management

Other books in the series (continued):

Harvard Business Review on Decision Making

Harvard Business Review on Developing Leaders

Harvard Business Review on Doing Business in China

Harvard Business Review on Effective Communication

Harvard Business Review on Entrepreneurship

Harvard Business Review on Finding and Keeping the Best People

Harvard Business Review on Innovation

Harvard Business Review on the Innovative Enterprise

Harvard Business Review on Knowledge Management

Harvard Business Review on Leadership

Harvard Business Review on Leadership at the Top

Harvard Business Review on Leadership in a Changed World

Harvard Business Review on Leading in Turbulent Times

Harvard Business Review on Managing Diversity

Harvard Business Review on Managing High-Tech Industries

Harvard Business Review on Managing People

Harvard Business Review on Managing Projects

Harvard Business Review on Managing Uncertainty

Harvard Business Review on Managing the Value Chain

Harvard Business Review on Managing Your Career

Harvard Business Review on Managing Yourself

Harvard Business Review on Marketing

Harvard Business Review on Measuring Corporate Performance

Harvard Business Review on Mergers and Acquisitions

Harvard Business Review on the Mind of the Leader

Harvard Business Review on Motivating People

Harvard Business Review on Negotiation and Conflict Resolution

Harvard Business Review on Nonprofits

Harvard Business Review on Organizational Learning

Harvard Business Review

ON

WOMEN IN BUSINESS

A HARVARD BUSINESS REVIEW PAPERBACK

The *Harvard Business Review* articles in this collection are available as
individual reprints. Discounts apply to quantity purchases. For information and ordering, please contact Customer Service, Harvard Business
School Publishing, Boston, MA 02163. Telephone: (617) 783-7500 or
(800) 988-0886, 8 A.M. to 6 P.M. Eastern Time, Monday through Friday.
Fax: (617) 783-7555, 24 hours a day. E-mail: custserv@hbsp.harvard.edu.

978-1-59139-717-5 (ISBN 13)
Library of Congress Cataloging-in-Publication Data
Harvard business review on women in business.
        p. cm. — (The Harvard business review paperback series)
        Includes index.
        ISBN 1-59139-717-0
        1. Women in the professions. Women executives. 3. Business-
women. 4. Women—Employment re-entry. 5. Career development. 6.
Work and family 7. Achievement motivation. I. Harvard business
review. II. Series.
HD6054.H366 2005
331.4'25—dc22   2005017056

Contents

Harvard
Business
Review

ON
WOMEN IN BUSINESS

Off-Ramps and On-Ramps

Keeping Talented Women on the Road to Success

SYLVIA ANN HEWLETT AND

CAROLYN BUCK LUCE

Executive Summary

MOST PROFESSIONAL WOMEN step off the career fast track at some point. With children to raise, elderly parents to care for, and other pulls on their time, these women are confronted with one off-ramp after another. When they feel pushed at the same time by long hours and unsatisfying work, the decision to leave becomes even easier. But woe to the woman who intends for that exit to be temporary. The on-ramps for professional women to get back on track are few and far between, the authors confirm. Their new survey research reveals for the first time the extent of the problem—what percentage of highly qualified women leave work and for how long, what obstacles they face coming back, and what price they pay for their time-outs.

And what are the implications for corporate America? One thing at least seems clear: As market and economic factors align in ways guaranteed to make talent constraints and skill shortages huge issues again, employers must learn to reverse this brain drain. Like it or not, large numbers of highly qualified, committed women need to take time out of the workplace. The trick is to help them maintain connections that will allow them to reenter the workforce without being marginalized for the rest of their lives.

Strategies for building such connections include creating reduced-hour jobs, providing flexibility in the workday and in the arc of a career, removing the stigma of taking time off, refusing to burn bridges, offering outlets for altruism, and nurturing women's ambition. An HBR Special Report, available online at www.womenscareersreport .hbr.org, presents detailed findings of the survey.

THROUGHOUT THE PAST YEAR, a noisy debate has erupted in the media over the meaning of what Lisa Belkin of the *New York Times* has called the "opt-out revolution." Recent articles in the *Wall Street Journal*, the *New York Times, Time,* and *Fast Company* all point to a disturbing trend—large numbers of highly qualified women dropping out of mainstream careers. These articles also speculate on what might be behind this new brain drain. Are the complex demands of modern child rearing the nub of the problem? Or should one blame the trend on a failure of female ambition?

The facts and figures in these articles are eye-catching: a survey of the class of 1981 at Stanford University showing that 57% of women graduates leave the work force; a survey of three graduating classes at Harvard Business School demonstrating that only 38% of women graduates end up in full-time careers; and a broader-gauged study of

MBAs showing that one in three white women holding an MBA is not working full-time, compared with one in 20 for men with the same degree.

The stories that enliven these articles are also powerful: Brenda Barnes, the former CEO of PepsiCo, who gave up her megawatt career to spend more time with her three children; Karen Hughes, who resigned from her enormously influential job in the Bush White House to go home to Texas to better look after a needy teenage son; and a raft of less prominent women who also said goodbye to their careers. Lisa Beattie Frelinghuysen, for example—featured in a recent *60 Minutes* segment—was building a very successful career as a lawyer. She'd been president of the law review at Stanford and went to work for a prestigious law firm. She quit after she had her first baby three years later.

These stories certainly resonate, but scratch the surface and it quickly becomes clear that there is very little in the way of systematic, rigorous data about the seeming exodus. A sector here, a graduating class there, and a flood of anecdotes: No one seems to know the basic facts. Across professions and across sectors, what is the scope of this opt-out phenomenon? What proportion of professional women take off-ramps rather than continue on their chosen career paths? Are they pushed off or pulled? Which sectors of the economy are most severely affected when women leave the workforce? How many years do women tend to spend out of the workforce? When women decide to reenter, what are they looking for? How easy is it to find on-ramps? What policies and practices help women return to work?

Early in 2004, the Center for Work-Life Policy formed a private sector, multiyear task force entitled "The Hidden Brain Drain: Women and Minorities as Unrealized Assets" to answer these and other questions. In the summer of 2004, three member companies of the task force (Ernst & Young, Goldman Sachs, and Lehman Brothers) sponsored a survey specifically designed to investigate the role of off-ramps and on-ramps in the lives of highly qualified women. The survey, conducted by Harris Interactive, comprised a nationally representative group of highly qualified women, defined as those with a graduate degree, a professional degree, or a high-honors undergraduate degree. The sample size was 2,443 women. The survey focused on two age groups: older women aged 41 to 55 and younger women aged 28 to 40. We also surveyed a smaller group of highly qualified men (653) to allow us to draw comparisons.

Using the data from the survey, we've created a more comprehensive and nuanced portrait of women's career paths than has been available to date. Even more important, these data suggest actions that companies can take to ensure that female potential does not go unrealized. Given current demographic and labor market trends, it's imperative that employers learn to reverse this brain drain. Indeed, companies that can develop policies and practices to tap into the female talent pool over the long haul will enjoy a substantial competitive advantage.

Women Do Leave

Many women take an off-ramp at some point on their career highway. Nearly four in ten highly qualified women (37%) report that they have left work voluntarily at some point in their careers. Among women who have children, that statistic rises to 43%.

Factors other than having children that pull women away from their jobs include the demands of caring for elderly parents or other family members (reported by 24%) and personal health issues (9%). Not surprisingly, the pull of elder care responsibilities is particularly strong for women in the 41 to 55 age group—often called the "sandwich" generation, positioned as it is between growing children and aging parents. One in three women in that bracket have left work for some period to spend time caring for family members who are not children. And lurking behind all this is the pervasiveness of a highly traditional division of labor on the home front. In a 2001 survey conducted by the Center for Work-Life Policy, fully 40% of highly qualified women with spouses felt that their husbands create more work around the house than they perform.

Alongside these "pull" factors are a series of "push" factors—that is, features of the job or workplace that make women head for the door. Seventeen percent of women say they took an off-ramp, at least in part, because their jobs were not satisfying or meaningful. Overall, understimulation and lack of opportunity seem to be larger problems than overwork. Only 6% of women stopped working because the work itself was too demanding. In business sectors, the survey results suggest that push factors are particularly powerful—indeed, in these sectors, unlike, say, in medicine or teaching, they outweigh pull factors. Of course, in the hurly-burly world of everyday life, most women are dealing with a combination of push and pull factors—and one often serves to intensify the other. When women feel hemmed in by rigid policies or a glass ceiling, for example, they are much more likely to respond to the pull of family.

It's important to note that, however pulled or pushed, only a relatively privileged group of women have the option of not working. Most women cannot quit their careers unless their spouses earn considerable incomes. Fully 32% of the women surveyed cite the fact that their spouses' income "was sufficient for our family to live on one income" as a reason contributing to their decision to off-ramp.

Contrast this with the experience of highly qualified men, only 24% of whom have taken off-ramps (with no statistical difference between those who are fathers and those who are not). When men leave the workforce, they do it for different reasons. Child-care and elder-care responsibilities are much less important; only 12% of men cite these factors as compared with 44% of women. Instead, on the pull side, they cite switching careers (29%), obtaining additional training (25%), or starting a business (12%) as important reasons for taking time out. For highly qualified men, off-ramping seems to be about strategic repositioning in their careers—a far cry from the dominant concerns of their female peers.

For many women in our study, the decision to off-ramp is a tough one. These women have invested heavily in their education and training. They have spent years accumulating the skills and credentials necessary for successful careers. Most are not eager to toss that painstaking effort aside. See the exhibit "How Many Opt Out?" for more information.

Lost on Reentry

Among women who take off-ramps, the overwhelming majority have every intention of returning to the work-force—and seemingly little idea of just how difficult that will prove. Women, like lawyer Lisa Beattie Frelinghuy-sen from the *60 Minutes* segment, who happily give up their careers to have children are the exception rather than the rule. In our research, we find that most highly qualified women who are currently off-ramped (93%) want to return to their careers.

Many of these women have financial reasons for wanting to get back to work. Nearly half (46%) cite "having their own independent source of income" as an important propelling factor. Women who participated in focus groups conducted as part of our research talked about their discomfort with "dependence." However good their marriages, many disliked needing to ask for money. Not being able to splurge on some small extravagance or make their own philanthropic choices without clearing it with their husbands did not sit well with them. It's also true that a significant proportion of women currently seeking on-ramps are facing troubling shortfalls in family income: 38% cite "household income no longer sufficient for family needs" and 24% cite

---

How Many Opt Out?

In our survey of highly qualified professionals, we asked the question, "Since you first began working, has there ever been a period where you took a voluntary time out from work?" Nearly four in ten women reported that they had—and that statistic rises to 43% among women who have children. By contrast, only 24% of highly qualified men have taken off-ramps (with no statistical difference between those who are fathers and those who are not).

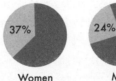

Women   Men

"partner's income no longer sufficient for family needs."
Given what has happened to the cost of homes (up 38%
over the past five years), the cost of college education (up
40% over the past decade), and the cost of health insurance (up 49% since 2000), it's easy to see why many professional families find it hard to manage on one income.

But financial pressure does not tell the whole story.
Many of these women find deep pleasure in their chosen
careers and want to reconnect with something they love.
Forty-three percent cite the "enjoyment and satisfaction"
they derive from their careers as an important reason to
return—among teachers this figure rises to 54% and
among doctors it rises to 70%. A further 16% want to
"regain power and status in their profession." In our
focus groups, women talked eloquently about how work
gives shape and structure to their lives, boosts confidence and self-esteem, and confers status and standing
in their communities. For many off-rampers, their professional identities remain their primary identities,
despite the fact that they have taken time out.

Perhaps most interesting, 24% of the women currently looking for on-ramps are motivated by "a desire to
give something back to society" and are seeking jobs that
allow them to contribute to their communities in some
way. In our focus groups, off-ramped women talked
about how their time at home had changed their aspirations. Whether they had gotten involved in protecting
the wetlands, supporting the local library, or rebuilding a
playground, they felt newly connected to the importance
of what one woman called "the work of care."

Unfortunately, only 74% of off-ramped women who
want to rejoin the ranks of the employed manage to do
so, according to our survey. And among these, only 40%

return to full-time, professional jobs. Many (24%) take part-time jobs, and some (9%) become self-employed. The implication is clear: Off-ramps are around every curve in the road, but once a woman has taken one, on-ramps are few and far between—and extremely costly. See the exhibit "Why Do They Leave the Fast Lane?" for more information.

Why Do They Leave the Fast Lane?

Our survey data show that women and men take off-ramps for dramatically different reasons. While men leave the workforce mainly to reposition themselves for a career change, the majority of women off-ramp to attend to responsibilities at home.

**Top Five Reasons Women
Leave the Fast Lane**

Family time	44%
Earn a degree, other training	23%
Work not enjoyable/satisfying	17%
Moved away	17%
Change careers	16%

**Top Five Reasons Men
Leave the Fast Lane**

Change careers	29%
Earn a degree, other training	25%
Work not enjoyable/satisfying	24%
Not interested in field	18%
Family time	12%

The Penalties of Time Out

Women off-ramp for surprisingly short periods of time—
on average, 2.2 years. In business sectors, off-rampers
average even shorter periods of time out (1.2 years).
However, even these relatively short career interruptions
entail heavy financial penalties. Our data show that
women lose an average of 18% of their earning power
when they take an off-ramp. In business sectors, penalties are particularly draconian: In these fields, women's
earning power dips an average of 28% when they take
time out. The longer you spend out, the more severe the
penalty becomes. Across sectors, women lose a stagger-
ing 37% of their earning power when they spend three or
more years out of the workforce.

Naomi, 34, is a case in point. In an interview, this
part-time working mother was open about her anxieties:
"Every day, I think about what I am going to do when I
want to return to work full-time. I worry about whether I
will be employable—will anyone even look at my
résumé?" This is despite an MBA and substantial work
experience.

Three years ago, Naomi felt she had no choice but to
quit her lucrative position in market research. She had
just had a child, and returning to full-time work after the
standard maternity leave proved to be well-nigh impossible. Her 55-hour week combined with her husband's 80-
hour week didn't leave enough time to raise a healthy
child—let alone care for a child who was prone to illness,
as theirs was. When her employer denied her request to
work reduced hours, Naomi quit.

After nine months at home, Naomi did find some flexible work—but it came at a high price. Her new freelance
job as a consultant to an advertising agency barely cov-

ered the cost of her son's day care. She now earns a third of what she did three years ago. What plagues Naomi the most about her situation is her anxiety about the future. "Will my skills become obsolete? Will I be able to support myself and my son if something should happen to my husband?"

The scholarly literature shows that Naomi's experience is not unusual. Economist Jane Waldfogel has analyzed the pattern of earnings over the life span. When women enter the workforce in their early and mid twenties they earn nearly as much as men do. For a few years, they almost keep pace. For example, at ages 25 to 29, they earn 87% of the male wage. However, when women start having children, their earnings fall way behind those of men. By the time they reach the 40-to-44 age group, women earn a mere 71% of the male wage. In the words of MIT economist Lester Thurow, "These are the prime years for establishing a successful career. These are the years when hard work has the maximum payoff. They are also the prime years for launching a family. Women who leave the job market during those years may find that they never catch up." See the exhibit "The High Cost of Time Out" for more information.

Taking the Scenic Route

A majority (58%) of highly qualified women describe their careers as "nonlinear"—which is to say, they do not follow the conventional trajectory long established by successful men. That ladder of success features a steep gradient in one's 30s and steady progress thereafter. In contrast, these women report that their "career paths have not followed a progression through the hierarchy of an industry."

Some of this nonlinearity is the result of taking off-ramps. But there are many other ways in which women ease out of the professional fast lane. Our survey reveals that 16% of highly qualified women work part-time. Such arrangements are more prevalent in the legal and medical professions, where 23% and 20% of female professionals work less than full-time, than in the business sector, where only 8% of women work part-time. Another common work-life strategy is telecommuting; 8% of highly qualified women work exclusively from home, and another 25% work partly from home.

The High Cost of Time Out

Though the average amount of time that women take off from their careers is surprisingly short (less than three years), the salary penalty for doing so is severe. Women who return to the workforce after time out earn significantly less than their peers who remained in their jobs.

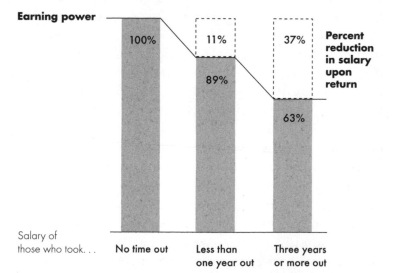

Earning power

100%   11%   37%   **Percent reduction in salary upon return**

89%

63%

Salary of those who took. . .   **No time out**   **Less than one year out**   **Three years or more out**

Looking back over their careers, 36% of highly qualified women say they have worked part-time for some
period of time as part of a strategy to balance work and
personal life. Twenty-five percent say they have reduced
the number of work hours within a full-time job, and
16% say they have declined a promotion. A significant
proportion (38%) say they have deliberately chosen a
position with fewer responsibilities and lower compensation than they were qualified for, in order to fulfill
responsibilities at home.

Downsizing Ambition

Given the tour of women's careers we've just taken, is it
any surprise that women find it difficult to claim or sustain ambition? The survey shows that while almost half
of the men consider themselves extremely or very ambitious, only about a third of the women do. (The proportion rises among women in business and the professions
of law and medicine; there, 43% and 51%, respectively,
consider themselves very ambitious.) In a similar vein,
only 15% of highly qualified women (and 27% in the business sector) single out "a powerful position" as an important career goal; in fact, this goal ranked lowest in
women's priorities in every sector we surveyed.

Far more important to these women are other items
on the workplace wish list: the ability to associate with
people they respect (82%); the freedom to "be themselves" at work (79%); and the opportunity to be flexible
with their schedules (64%). Fully 61% of women consider
it extremely or very important to have the opportunity to
collaborate with others and work as part of a team. A
majority (56%) believe it is very important for them to be

able to give back to the community through their work. And 51% find "recognition from my company" either extremely or very important.

These top priorities constitute a departure from the traditional male take on ambition. Moreover, further analysis points to a disturbing age gap. In the business sector, 53% of younger women (ages 28 to 40) own up to being very ambitious, as contrasted with only 37% of older women. This makes sense in light of Anna Fels's groundbreaking work on women and ambition. In a 2004 HBR article, Fels argues convincingly that ambition stands on two legs—mastery and recognition. To hold onto their dreams, not only must women attain the necessary skills and experience, they must also have their achievements appropriately recognized. To the extent the latter is missing in female careers, ambition is undermined. A vicious cycle emerges: As women's ambitions stall, they are perceived as less committed, they no longer get the best assignments, and this lowers their ambitions further.

In our focus groups, we heard the disappointment—and discouragement—of women who had reached senior levels in corporations only to find the glass ceiling still in place, despite years of diversity initiatives. These women feel that they are languishing and have not been given either the opportunities or the recognition that would allow them to realize their full potential. Many feel handicapped in the attainment of their goals. The result is the vicious cycle that Fels describes: a "downsizing" of women's ambition that becomes a self-fulfilling prophecy. And the discrepancy in ambition levels between men and women has an insidious side effect in that it results in insufficient role models for younger women.

Reversing the Brain Drain

These, then, are the hard facts. With them in hand, we move from anecdotes to data—and, more important, to a different, richer analytical understanding of the problem. In the structural issue of off-ramps and on-ramps, we see the mechanism derailing the careers of highly qualified women and also the focal point for making positive change. What are the implications for corporate America? One thing at least seems clear: Employers can no longer pretend that treating women as "men in skirts" will fix their retention problems. Like it or not, large numbers of highly qualified, committed women need to take time out. The trick is to help them maintain connections that will allow them to come back from that time without being marginalized for the rest of their careers.

CREATE REDUCED-HOUR JOBS

The most obvious way to stay connected is to offer women with demanding lives a way to keep a hand in their chosen field, short of full-time involvement. Our survey found that, in business sectors, fully 89% of women believe that access to reduced-hour jobs is important. Across all sectors, the figure is 82%.

The Johnson & Johnson family of companies has seen the increased loyalty and productivity that can result from such arrangements. We recently held a focus group with 12 part-time managers at these companies and found a level of commitment that was palpable. The women had logged histories with J&J that ranged from eight to 19 years and spoke of the corporation with great affection. All had a focus on productivity and pushed themselves to deliver at the same level they had achieved before switching to part-time. One woman, a 15-year J&J veteran, was particularly eloquent in her gratitude to the corporation. She had had her first child at age 40 and, like so many new mothers, felt torn apart by the conflicting demands of home and work. In her words, "I thought I only had two choices—work full-time or leave—and I didn't want either. J&J's reduced-hour option has been a savior." All the women in the room were clear on one point: They would have quit had part-time jobs not been available.

At Pfizer, the deal is sweetened further for part-time workers; field sales professionals in the company's Vista Rx division are given access to the same benefits and training as full-time employees but work 60% of the hours (with a corresponding difference in base pay). Many opt for a three-day workweek; others structure their working day around children's school hours. These 230 employees—93% of whom are working mothers—remain eligible for promotion and may return to full-time status at their discretion.

PROVIDE FLEXIBILITY IN THE DAY

Some women don't require reduced work hours; they merely need flexibility in when, where, and how they do their work. Even parents who employ nannies or have children in day care, for example, must make time for teacher conferences, medical appointments, volunteering, child-related errands—not to mention the days the nanny calls in sick or the day care center is closed. Someone caring for an invalid or a fragile elderly person may likewise have many hours of potentially productive time in a day yet not be able to stray far from home.

For these and other reasons, almost two-thirds (64%) of the women we surveyed cite flexible work arrangements as being either extremely or very important to them. In fact, by a considerable margin, highly qualified women find flexibility more important than compensation; only 42% say that "earning a lot of money" is an important motivator. In our focus groups, we heard women use terms like "nirvana" and "the golden ring" to describe employment arrangements that allow them to flex their workdays, their workweeks, and their careers. A senior employee who recently joined Lehman Brothers' equity division is an example. She had been working at another financial services company when a Lehman recruiter called. "The person who had been in the job previously was working one day a week from home, so they offered that opportunity to me. Though I was content in my current job," she told us, "that intriguing possibility made me reevaluate. In the end, I took the job at Lehman. Working from home one day a week was a huge lure."

PROVIDE FLEXIBILITY IN THE ARC OF A CAREER

Booz Allen Hamilton, the management and technology consulting firm, recognized that it isn't simply a workday, or a workweek, that needs to be made more flexible. It's the entire arc of a career.

Management consulting as a profession loses twice as many women as men in the middle reaches of career ladders. A big part of the problem is that, perhaps more than in any other business sector, it is driven by an up-or-out ethos; client-serving professionals must progress steadily or fall by the wayside. The strongest contenders make partner through a relentless winnowing process. While many firms take care to make the separations as painless as possible (the chaff, after all, tends to land in organizations that might employ their services), there are clear limits to their patience. Typically, if a valued professional is unable to keep pace with the road warrior lifestyle, the best she can hope for is reassignment to a staff job.

Over the past year, Booz Allen has initiated a "ramp up, ramp down" flexible program to allow professionals to balance work and life and still do the client work they find most interesting. The key to the program is Booz Allen's effort to "unbundle" standard consulting projects and identify chunks that can be done by telecommuting or shorts stints in the office. Participating professionals are either regular employees or alumni that sign standard employment contracts and are activated as needed. For the professional, it's a way to take on a manageable amount of the kind of work they do best. For Booz Allen, it's a way to maintain ties to consultants who have already proved their merit in a challenging profession. Since many of these talented women will eventually return to full-time consulting employment, Booz Allen wants to be their employer of choice—and to keep their skills sharp in the meantime.

When asked how the program is being received, DeAnne Aguirre, a vice president at Booz Allen who was involved in its design (and who is also a member of our task force), had an instant reaction: "I think it's instilled new hope—a lot of young women I work with no longer feel that they will have to sacrifice some precious part of themselves." Aguirre explains that trade-offs are inevitable, but at Booz Allen an off-ramping decision doesn't have to be a devastating one anymore. "Flex careers are bound to be slower than conventional ones, but in ten years' time you probably won't remember the precise year you made partner. The point here is to remain on track and vitally connected."

REMOVE THE STIGMA

Making flexible arrangements succeed over the long term is hard work. It means crafting an imaginative set of policies, but even more important, it means eliminating the stigma that is often attached to such nonstandard work arrangements. As many as 35% of the women we surveyed report various aspects of their organizations' cultures that effectively penalize people who take advantage of work-life policies. Telecommuting appears to be most stigmatized, with 39% of women reporting some form of tacit resistance to it, followed by job sharing and part-time work. Of flexible work arrangements in general, 21% report that "there is an unspoken rule at my workplace that people who use these options will not be promoted." Parental leave policies get more respect—though even here, 19% of women report cultural or attitudinal barriers to taking the time off that they are entitled to. In environments where flexible work arrangements are tacitly deemed illegitimate, many women would rather resign than request them.

Interestingly, when it comes to taking advantage of work-life policies, men encounter even more stigma. For example, 48% of the men we surveyed perceived job sharing as illegitimate in their workplace culture—even when it's part of official policy.

Transformation of the corporate culture seems to be a prerequisite for success on the work-life front. Those people at or near the top of an organization need to have that "eureka" moment, when they not only understand the business imperative for imaginative work-life policies but are prepared to embrace them, and in so doing remove the stigma. In the words of Dessa Bokides, treasurer at Pitney Bowes, "Only a leader's devotion to these issues will give others permission to transform conventional career paths."

STOP BURNING BRIDGES

One particularly dramatic finding of our survey deserves special mention: Only 5% of highly qualified women looking for on-ramps are interested in rejoining the companies they left. In business sectors, that percentage is zero. If ever there was a danger signal for corporations, this is it.

The finding implies that the vast majority of off-ramped women, at the moment they left their careers, felt ill-used—or at least underutilized and unappreciated—by their employers. We can only speculate as to why this was. In some cases, perhaps, the situation ended badly; a woman, attempting impossible juggling feats, started dropping balls. Or an employer, embittered by the loss of too many "star" women, lets this one go much too easily.

It's understandable for managers to assume that women leave mainly for "pull" reasons and that there's no point in trying to keep them. Indeed, when family overload and the traditional division of labor place unmanageable demands on a working woman, it does appear that quitting has much more to do with what's going on at home than what's going on at work. However, it is important to realize that even when pull factors seem to be dominant, push factors are also in play. Most off-ramping decisions are conditioned by policies, practices, and attitudes at work. Recognition, flexibility, and the opportunity to telecommute—especially when endorsed by the corporate culture—can make a huge difference.

The point is, managers will not stay in a departing employee's good graces unless they take the time to explore the reasons for off-ramping and are able and willing to offer options short of total severance. If a company wants future access to this talent, it will need to go beyond the perfunctory exit interview and, at the very least, impart the message that the door is open. Better still, it will maintain a connection with off-ramped employees through a formal alumni program.

PROVIDE OUTLETS FOR ALTRUISM

Imaginative attachment policies notwithstanding, some women have no interest in returning to their old organizations because their desire to work in their former field has waned. Recall the focus group participants who spoke of a deepened desire to give back to the community after taking a hiatus from work. Remember, too, that women in business sectors are pushed off track more by dissatisfaction with work than pulled by external demands. Our data suggest that fully 52% of women with MBAs in the business sector cite the fact that they do not find their careers "either satisfying or enjoyable" as an important reason for why they left work. Perhaps not surprisingly, then, a majority (54%) of the women looking for on-ramps want to change their profession or field. And in most of those cases, it's a woman who formerly worked in the corporate sphere hoping to move into the not-for-profit sector.

Employers would be well advised to recognize and harness the altruism of these women. Supporting female professionals in their advocacy and public service efforts serves to win their energy and loyalty. Companies may also be able to redirect women's desire to give back to the community by asking them to become involved in mentoring and formal women's networks within the company.

NURTURE AMBITION

Finally, if women are to sustain their passion for work and their competitive edge—whether or not they take formal time out—they must keep ambition alive. Our findings point to an urgent need to implement mentoring and networking programs that help women expand and sustain their professional aspirations. Companies like American Express, GE, Goldman Sachs, Johnson & Johnson, Lehman Brothers, and Time Warner are developing "old girls networks" that build skills, contacts, and confidence. They link women to inside power brokers and to outside business players and effectively inculcate those precious rainmaking skills.

Networks (with fund-raising and friend-raising functions) can enhance client connections. But they also play another, critical role. They provide the infrastructure within which women can earn recognition, as well as a safe platform from which to blow one's own horn without being perceived as too pushy. In the words of Patricia Fili-Krushel, executive vice president of Time Warner, "Company-sponsored women's networks encourage women to cultivate both sides of the power equation. Women hone their own leadership abilities but also learn to use power on behalf of others. Both skill sets help us increase our pipeline of talented women."

Adopt an On-Ramp

As we write this, market and economic factors, both cyclical and structural, are aligned in ways guaranteed to make talent constraints and skill shortages huge issues again. Unemployment is down and labor markets are beginning to tighten, just as the baby-bust generation is about to hit "prime time" and the number of workers between the ages of 35 to 45 is shrinking. Immigration levels are stable, so there's little chance of relief there. Likewise, productivity improvements are flattening. The phenomenon that bailed us out of our last big labor crunch—the entry for the first time of millions of women into the labor force—is not available to us again. Add it all up, and CEOs are back to wondering how they will find enough high-caliber talent to drive growth.

There is a winning strategy. It revolves around the retention and reattachment of highly qualified women. America these days has a large and impressive pool of female talent. Fifty-eight percent of college graduates are now women, and nearly half of all professional and graduate degrees are earned by women. Even more important, the incremental additions to the talent pool will be disproportionately female, according to figures released by the U.S. Department of Education. The number of women with graduate and professional degrees is projected to grow by 16% over the next decade, while the number of men with these degrees is projected to grow by a mere 1.3%. Companies are beginning to pay attention to these figures. As Melinda Wolfe, head of global leadership and diversity at Goldman Sachs, recently pointed out, "A large part of the potential talent pool consists of females and historically underrepresented groups. With the professional labor market tightening, it is in our direct interest to give serious attention to these matters of retention and reattachment."

In short, the talent is there; the challenge is to create the circumstances that allow businesses to take advantage of it over the long run. To tap this all-important resource, companies must understand the complexities of women's nonlinear careers and be prepared to support rather than punish those who take alternate routes.

How Ernst & Young Keeps Women on the Path to Partnership

IN THE MID-1990s, turnover among female employees at Ernst & Young was much higher than it was among male peers. Company leaders knew something was seriously wrong; for many years, its entering classes of young auditors had been made up of nearly equal numbers of men and women—yet it was still the case that only a tiny percentage of its partnership was female. This was a major problem. Turnover in client-serving roles meant lost continuity on work assignments. And on top of losing talent that the firm had invested in training, E&Y was incurring costs averaging 150% of a departing employee's annual salary just to fill the vacant position.

E&Y set a new course, marked by several important features outlined here. Since E&Y began this work, the percentage of women partners has more than tripled to 12% and the downward trend in retention of women at every level has been reversed. E&Y now has four women on the management board, and many more women are in key operating and client serving roles. Among its women partners, 10% work on a flexible schedule and more than 20 have been promoted to partner while working a reduced schedule. In 2004, 22% of new partners were women.

Focus

Regional pilot projects targeted five areas for improvement: Palo Alto and San Jose focused on life balance, Minneapolis on mentoring, New Jersey on flexible work arrangements, Boston on women networking in the business community, and Washington, DC, on women networking inside E&Y. Successful solutions were rolled out across the firm.

Committed Leadership

Philip Laskawy, E&Y's chairman from 1994 to 2001, made it a priority to retain and promote women. He convened a diversity task force of partners to focus on the problem and created an Office of Retention. Laskawy's successor, Jim Turley, deepened the focus on diversity by rolling out a People First strategy.

Policies

Ernst & Young equipped all its people for telework and made it policy that flexible work schedules would not affect anyone's opportunity for advancement. The new premise was that all jobs could be done flexibly.

New Roles

E&Y's Center for the New Workforce dedicates its staff of seven to developing and advancing women into leadership roles. A strategy team of three professionals addresses the firm's flexibility goals for both men and women. Also, certain partners are designated as "career watchers" and track individual women's progress, in particular, monitoring the caliber of the projects and clients to which they are assigned.

Learning Resources

All employees can use E&Y's Achieving Flexibility Web site to learn about flexible work arrangements. They can track how certain FWAs were negotiated and structured and can use the contact information provided in the database to ask those employees questions about how it is (or isn't) working.

Peer Networking

Professional Women's Networks are active in 41 offices, and they focus on building the skills, confidence, leadership opportunities, and networks necessary for women to be successful. A three-day Women's Leadership Conference is held every 18 months. The most recent was attended by more than 425 women partners, principals, and directors.

Accountability

The annual People Point survey allows employees to rate managers on how well they foster an inclusive, flexible work environment. Managers are also evaluated on metrics like number of women serving key accounts, in key leadership jobs, and in the partner pipeline.

Notes

1. The complete statistical findings from this research project, and additional commentary and company examples, are available in an HBR research report entitled "The Hidden Brain Drain: Off-Ramps and On-Ramps in Women's Careers" (see *www.womenscareersreport.hbr.org*).

Originally published in January 2005
Reprint R0503B

The New Road to the Top

PETER CAPPELLI AND MONIKA HAMORI

Executive Summary

BY COMPARING THE TOP EXECUTIVES of 1980's *Fortune* 100 companies with the top brass of firms in the 2001 list, the authors have quantified a transformation that until now has been largely anecdotal. A dramatic shift in executive careers, and in executives themselves, has occurred over the past two decades. Today's *Fortune* 100 executives are younger, more of them are female, and fewer were educated at elite institutions. They're also making their way to the top more quickly. They're taking fewer jobs along the way, and they increasingly move from one company to the next as their careers unfold.

In their wide-ranging analysis, the authors offer a number of insights. For one thing, it has become clear that there are huge advantages to working in a growing firm. For another, the firms that have been big for a long time still provide the most extensive training and development. They also offer relatively long promotion ladders—hence the common wisdom that these "academy companies" are great to have been *from*.

While women were disproportionately scarce among the most senior ranks of executives in 2001, those who arrived got there faster and at a younger age than their male colleagues. Perhaps the career hurdles that women face had blocked all but the most highly qualified female managers, who then proceeded to rise quickly.

In the future, a record of good P&L performance may become even more critical to getting hired and advancing in the largest companies. As a result, we may see a reversal of the usual flow of talent, which has been from the academy companies to smaller firms. It may be increasingly common for executives to develop records of performance in small companies, or even as entrepreneurs, and then seek positions in large corporations.

FROM THE 1950S THROUGH THE 1970S, American executives looked a lot alike. They tended to be model organization men (indeed, they were virtually all male) who stuck faithfully with the companies that first hired them, and they climbed methodically up the corporate ladder until, at last, they retired.

The dominant notion during this time was that a business career ran its course *inside* a corporation. William H. Whyte, the *Fortune* magazine editor whose 1956 classic book *The Organization Man* made the phrase famous, asked what was seen at the time as a novel question: Why would executives ever leave their firms? He cited a Booz Allen study showing that executives only left their first employers if the companies could not deliver on their implicit promise of upward mobility. Then in the 1960s and 1970s, the intricate details of real careers were mapped out in a series of studies such as Rosabeth Moss Kanter's famous account of inbreeding at the pseudonymous "Indsco" corporation. There were hints throughout the 1970s that things were changing. But for the most part, the question of whether executive careers had altered in any significant way would not be rigorously examined for more than a decade.

Our research puts executive careers under the microscope once again. In a study comparing *Fortune* 100 executives in 1980 with their counterparts in 2001, we have quantified a transformation that until now has been largely anecdotal. While executives in 1980 looked pretty much like those in previous decades, a dramatic shift in careers, and in executives themselves, began in the years after 1980. Today's top managers of *Fortune* 100 companies are fundamentally different: They are younger, more of them are female, and fewer of them were educated at elite institutions. They're making it to the top faster and taking fewer jobs along the way. And they are increasingly moving from one company to another as their careers unfold.

In this article, we'll describe our study and highlight its key findings. And we'll examine what the transformed environment means for executives who are mapping out careers in this newly charted territory.

How Has the *Fortune* 100 Changed?

Before we present our findings on how executives and their career tracks changed between 1980 and 2001, it's important that we explore how the *Fortune* 100 itself transformed during that period. Changes in the size, age, and management structure of the companies, as well as the list's industry concentration, contributed to the evolution of executive careers.

Although the *Fortune* 100 comprises the most stable corporations in the world, there has been considerable churn in the list. Only 26% of the companies on it in 1980 were still there in 2001. (For a breakdown, see the exhibit "Turnover at the Top.")

The changes in the *Fortune* 100's makeup dramatically highlight the continuing shift in the United States toward a service economy. The decline of manufacturing on the list and the rise of financial services are especially striking. (For a summary of the changes in the list's makeup, see the exhibit "A Shifting Industry Mix.")

Despite turmoil in the economy over the past two decades, the *Fortune* 100 companies in 2001 were significantly older, on average, than the firms on the list in 1980. Their sales revenues were also much higher—the companies' combined sales rose fourfold in a period when U.S. prices rose 115%. Despite this expansion, average employment in these companies grew by only 24%. For more information, see the exhibits "Turnover at the Top," "A Shifting Industry Mix," and "Compared with *Fortune* 100 Companies . . ."

How Have *Fortune* 100 Executives Changed?

With a clear picture of how the characteristics of the *Fortune* 100 have changed, we turn now to the attributes and career experiences of executives holding top positions. We examined age, gender, promotions, years of education, nature and number of educational institutions attended, tenure within companies, and the time it took executives to achieve their positions. Like the *Fortune* 100 itself, *Fortune* 100 executives have undergone a transformation in the last two decades.

While women filled just 11% of executive positions in 2001, that's a substantial improvement; in 1980, the figure was zero. The women who joined the *Fortune* 100 executive ranks differed from their male counterparts. They were significantly younger; they were less likely to have been lifetime employees; they spent less time, on average, in each of their jobs; and they got to the executive ranks much faster.

The average *Fortune* 100 top executive in 2001 was more than four years younger than the top executive in

---

Turnover at the Top

Only 26% of companies in the 2001 Fortune 100 were also on the 1980 list.

**Fortune 100
Companies in 2001**

Boeing	Honeywell
Caterpiller	IBM
Chevron	International Paper
Coca-Cola	Johnson & Johnson
Conoco	Lockheed Martin
Dow Chemical	Marathon Oil
DuPont	PepsiCo
Exxon Mobil	Philip Morris
Ford	Phillips Petroleum
General Electric	Procter & Gamble
General Mills	Texaco (became
General Motors	ChevronTexaco in 2001)
Georgia-Pacific	Union Pacific
	United Technologies

A Shifting Industry Mix

Percentage of Fortune *100 executives in each industry*

Industry	1980	2001
Aerospace	7.4	4.2
Agriculture	1.1	0
Automotive	6.9	2.4
Business services	0.6	0.9
Chemicals	6.0	3.2
Communications	3.4	9.1
Computers	2.6	8.9
Construction	0.6	0
Consumer products	0	0.9
Electric utilities	5.7	5.4
Energy	20.4	12.8
Entertainment	0	0.3
Financial services	0	16.6
Food	12.0	4.7
Health care	0.7	5.3
Insurance	0	5.9
Manufacturing	17.3	1.1
Paper	4.5	2.1
Photography	1.0	0
Retail	2.6	14.4
Steel	5.4	0.7
Transportation	1.7	0
Wholesale trade	0	1.0

1980 and slightly more educated, at least as measured by years in school. (The higher level of education corresponds to an increase in education for the general population during this period.) The nature of their education changed more dramatically: In 1980, undergraduate degrees from Ivy League and other elite schools were relatively common; by 2001, the importance of an elite education had clearly fallen, and companies had opened their doors to candidates from public schools.

How Have the Experiences of *Fortune* 100 Executives Changed?

Executives are moving up faster than they once did. The journey from first job to executive suite is shorter—by four years, on average—than it was a generation ago, and it involves fewer stops along the way. Though executives stay on each rung nearly as long as they used to, today's

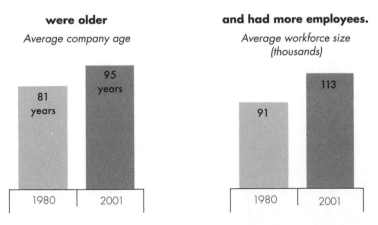

Compared with Fortune 100 Companies in 1980, those in 2001 . . .

were older	and had more employees.
Average company age	Average workforce size (thousands)

81 years (1980) — 95 years (2001)

91 (1980) — 113 (2001)

career ladder seems to have fewer rungs, and they're spaced farther apart. That is, the average promotion entails a greater leap in responsibility. This trend is consistent with the widespread perception that corporate hierarchies are flattening.

We also found that executives aren't staying put the way they once did. There was an eight-point decline between 1980 and 2001 in the percentage of top executives who spent their entire careers at the same companies. A related statistic, average tenure for these executives in their companies, dropped by more than five years (median tenure, which is less sensitive to extreme values, dropped even more, by 7.5 years).

Finally, we measured a considerable change in the distribution of executives by job responsibility between 1980 and 2001. Not all companies have exactly the same hierarchy of titles, but most have three tiers—CEO and chair level, executive vice president level, and vice president level. Thus, changes in the percentages of individuals in each tier are more revealing than changes in titles. We found that the percentages in the top and middle tiers declined, while the percentage in the lower tier expanded substantially, again supporting the perception that corporate hierarchies have become flatter.

What Are the Career Implications?

Some of the most important lessons from our study and related work by other researchers derive from the finding that different types of firms offer different prospects for advancement. It's clear, for instance, that there are huge advantages to working in a growing firm. Executives are much more likely to be promoted in firms with healthy growth rates than in stagnating companies. (See the exhibit "Speed to Top Depends on Industry".) Further evidence from the data suggests that, other things being equal, younger firms offer faster advancement, perhaps because of their tendency to have flatter hierarchies.

The firms that have been big for a long time—those in the *Fortune* 100 in 1980 and again in 2001—seem to handle career advancement and development differently from others. General Electric, Procter & Gamble, and the like provide extensive training and development opportunities. They also offer relatively long promotion ladders—hence the common notion that these "academy companies" are great to have been *from*. They are faster moving and leaner than they were in 1980, but they still offer greater stability and predictability than other large corporations and so are very attractive for some people, not only as a place to begin a career but as a place to complete one. Younger companies and restructuring firms may offer great opportunities for rapid advancement, but those opportunities come with uncertainty—you could be in line for a top job and see your career derailed by a reorganization.

The irony is that while the academy companies remain the gold standard for career management, fewer and fewer corporations appear to be following that model. We wonder whether academy companies are simply the last to change or whether in 20 years, the *Fortune* 100 will still include companies that make extensive investments in their managers and executives.

Inside Strategies

Another set of lessons concerns what happens to executives inside companies. Prior research suggested that

Speed to Top Depends on Industry

Our current research, as well as previous work by others, suggests that companies in fast-growing industries offer better prospects for advancement. For example, the two industries offering executives the fastest paths to the top in 2001 were wholesale trade and financial services, industries that had no companies big enough to be in the Fortune *100 in 1980.*

More important, however, are data showing that in both 1980 and 2001, executives reached the top more quickly in industries that were undergoing structural change. These industries were built on emerging or quickly changing technologies or required new competencies—and therefore needed a new generation of executives. Consider the steel industry, which in 1980 was one of the most stable. Executives advanced slowly, taking almost 31 years to rise to the top. Steel was certainly not a growth industry from 1980 to 2001. But it has been wracked by consolidations and restructurings that have created promotion opportunities for executives with different skills. By 2001, steel offered one of the fastest paths to the top—23.6 years.

Executives' Mean Time to Top, by Industry

In years, ranked from greatest decrease to greatest increase

Industry	1980	2001	Change
Steel	31	23.6	–7.4
Business services	32	25.5	–6.5
Electric utilities	28.5	23.7	–4.8
Communications	28.2	24.4	–3.8
Health care	27	23.2	–3.8
Food	28.7	25.2	–3.5
Energy	28.4	26	–2.4
Chemicals	28.6	26.6	–2.0
Aerospace	29.7	27.8	–1.9
Computers	25.8	25	–0.8
Retail	23.9	23.8	–0.1
Manufacturing	28.5	28.8	+0.3
Automotive	28.4	29	+0.6
Paper	26.1	28.4	+2.3
Industries that weren't on the *Fortune* 100 in 1980			
Wholesale trade	—	21.6	—
Financial services	—	22.7	—
Insurance	—	23.6	—
Consumer products	—	26.3	—
Entertainment	—	29.8	—

through the 1970s, marketing was the preferred track into the executive suite, but the results here suggest that finance now offers by far the best path (it offered the best path in 1980, too, but consulting and—surprisingly—human resources were closer behind). The finance track will remain the dominant path to the C suite as long as the investor community wields a powerful influence on corporations.

Career research also offers insights about when it's best to move on. An individual's advancement may slow for reasons beyond his or her control, such as problems with immediate supervisors and changes in company strategies that reward different backgrounds. As the average age of executives in the highest jobs decreases, delays in promotions become more damaging to a manager's odds of getting to the top. An objective look at the company's prospects can help a manager decide whether to sit tight and hope the situation improves or move to a different company or division. Take a zero-based budgeting approach, as an investor would: If you were not already an employee, would you invest your human capital in this company, given its plans and current situation?

Another approach is to look around and ask, "Have I been here longer than others in this job?" If the answer is yes, this may be a good time to move on. Research suggests that the odds of advancement fall as a person's tenure in a job grows. Individuals who advance to the top tend to be among the youngest in their cohorts—possibly because talent and ability get spotted early, possibly because of "halo" or reputation effects.

We think the most important finding in this study is that executives in 2001 got to the top faster than their 1980 counterparts and did so by holding fewer jobs along the way (see the earlier section "How Have the Experiences of *Fortune* 100 Executives Changed?"). But it may not necessarily follow that working for a company with few levels is the way to move up quickly. Anecdotal evidence suggests that such firms tend not to promote from within because they believe there's too great a gap in required competencies from rung to rung. So they hire from outside. Therefore, it may be easiest to move toward the top by doing well in a small company—as CFO, say—then taking the same job in a larger one. Another important point is that holding a general manager job with profit-and-loss responsibility seems to be a prerequisite for the highest positions, perhaps because the ability to run a business is considered transferable; success in running a $10 million organization is a powerful recommendation for a job running a $100 million organization.

But the data are not clear on whether people should jump from company to company to get ahead. Our 2001 findings show that executives who stayed in the same corporations for their entire careers got to the top as quickly as their firm-hopping colleagues—a change from the situation a generation ago—but far fewer executives are spending their careers in one company. So perhaps only those who are advancing quickly choose to stay put.

Women in the Executive Suite

For female executives, the data are both discouraging and encouraging. While women were disproportionately scarce among the most senior executives in 2001—and scarcer still in CEO jobs—those who arrived got there faster and at a younger age than their male colleagues. We're not sure why these women, so few in number, progressed so quickly toward the top. Perhaps they faced more career hurdles and were therefore more qualified than their male counterparts by the time they reached the executive suite.

If women had been distributed throughout the corporate suite as men were, we would have expected the percentage of female executives holding any given position to have been the same as the percentage of male executives. But women in the highest positions—CEOs, board chairs, vice chairs, and presidents—constituted only 10% of all the executive women in our 2001 survey, whereas men in those positions represented 25% of the male executives. The six female CEOs in the *Fortune* 100 were just 3% of the women; male CEOs made up 13% of the men.

Although women were largely excluded from the most senior positions, they were not relegated to the bottom. They disproportionately outnumbered men in important midtier positions such as senior vice president and executive vice president, and they were disproportionately outnumbered by men in lower executive positions such as vice president and group vice president.

The prevalence of female executives was fairly even across the categories of company size and company age, but not across industries. Women made up 32% of the top executives in health care, 25% in consumer products, and 17% in financial services. There were virtually no women executives in manufacturing, chemicals, entertainment, or wholesale trade (companies such as Costco). For certain industries, the disparity might be attributable to the numbers of women taking entry-level jobs 20 years ago—there were many female nurses, for example, and relatively few female chemical engineers. But there was no comparable disparity in entry-level jobs in the entertainment industry.

The huge gaps in the numbers of women executives in different industries suggest that systematic factors are at work, that some industries' cultures and practices make it feasible for women to advance while other industries' do not. But before women reject certain industries as inhospitable, they should bear in mind that restructuring could rapidly change their career prospects, just as restructuring in the steel industry opened opportunities for a new generation of executives with different skills. In considering job prospects, women would do better to evaluate an industry's overall stability rather than just its cultures and practices. See the exhibit "Women Join the Ranks of Top Execs" for more information.

Predictions for 2021

How will the top executives of 2021 compare with those of today? What factors will shape—indeed, are already

---

Women Join the Ranks of Top Execs

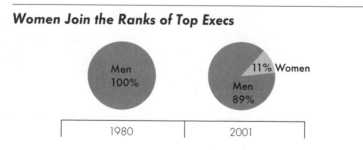

| 1980 | 2001 |

Younger, Faster, and More Mobile

Female Fortune 100 executives in 2001 differed from their male colleagues.

	Women	Men
Average age	47	52
Began career at current company	32%	47%
Average time in each job	3.4 years	4.0 years
Average time from first job to current position	21 years	25 years

shaping—their careers? Graduate training in business, especially the MBA degree, has in recent years become much more important for access to the best entry-level corporate jobs. It's a safe bet, therefore, that MBAs will be even more prominent in executive suites in the next generation. And the amount of job-hopping that young managers have already done suggests that by the time they enter the executive suite, they will have worked in many more organizations than their predecessors. The organizational tenures of top corporate executives will certainly decline.

Compared with Fortune 100 Executives in 1980, Those in 2001 . . .

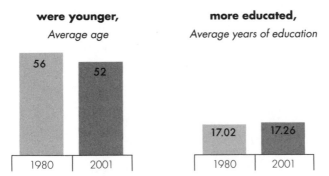

were younger,
Average age

more educated,
Average years of education

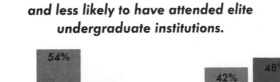

and less likely to have attended elite undergraduate institutions.

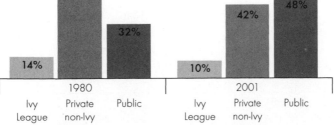

As corporations focus more intently on cutting costs and improving margins, expenditures for management development may be further trimmed. The most important experiences (and the hardest to get) will increasingly be those that involve hands-on responsibility for profit and loss. Big corporations are likely to become even more cautious about who they give this responsibility to. A record of good P&L performance may become even more critical to getting hired and advancing in the largest companies. As a result, we may see a reversal of the usual flow of talent, which has been from the academy companies to smaller firms. In the future, it may be more and more common for aspiring executives to develop performance records in small companies, or even as entrepreneurs, before moving to large corporations. If that happens, careers will have come full circle from the days when firms like DuPont and General Motors acquired new companies and placed the entrepreneurs who had founded them, people like Alfred Sloan, into newly created executive roles. For more information on how industries have already changed, please see the exhibits "Corporate Hierarchies Are Flattening," "Compared with Executives in 1980 . . . ," and "Young Firm, Old Firm."

Corporate Hierarchies Are Flattening

Percentage of executives holding job titles in the top, middle, and bottom tiers

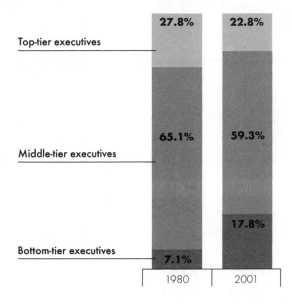

Compared with Executives in 1980, Executives in 2001 . . .

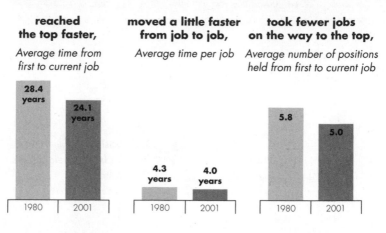

reached the top faster,

Average time from first to current job

1980	2001
28.4 years	24.1 years

moved a little faster from job to job,

Average time per job

1980	2001
4.3 years	4.0 years

took fewer jobs on the way to the top,

Average number of positions held from first to current job

1980	2001
5.8	5.0

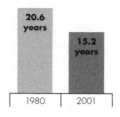

spent less time in their curent firms,

Average time in current company

1980	2001
20.6 years	15.2 years

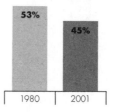

and were less likely to be "lifers."

Percentage of executives spending their entire careers in one company

1980	2001
53%	45%

Young Firm, Old Firm

We wondered whether the changes in company practices and executive attributes—reduced organizational tenure, faster promotions, lower executive age, and so on—represented new approaches to coprorate operations that were more likely to be characteristics of younger firms.

We compared younger firms in the 2001 Fortune 100—that is, corporations that had been in existence 30 years and less—with older firms on the list. Younger companies did have younger executives, perhaps not surprisingly, but they didn't have more women than the older corporations. And although we found slightly more public and fewer Ivy grads at younger firms, the education differences were not statistically significant. Executives in younger firms were far less likely to have begun their careers there, and their average organizational tenure was about half that of executives in older firms. Executives from younger companies also got to the top faster, apparently because they moved more frequently from company to company and because there were fewer steps in their promotion ladders. Although they spent about the same amount of time in each job as the executives in older firms, they held fewer positions before being promoted into the executive ranks. These results reinforce the prevalent perception that company age has an important influence on executive experiences and that the youngest firms—presumably the fastest growing—do the most recruiting of outside talent.

Compared with executives in older firms, those in younger firms . . .

were younger,

Average age of executives in firms that had existed for 30 years and less and in older firms

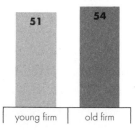

were less likely to be "lifers,"

Percentage of executives spending their entire careers in one company

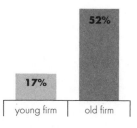

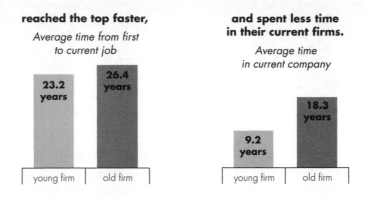

reached the top faster,

Average time from first to current job

23.2 years — young firm

26.4 years — old firm

and spent less time in their current firms.

Average time in current company

9.2 years — young firm

18.3 years — old firm

How the Study Was Done

WE FOCUSED ON *Fortune* 100 companies because they had the scale to manage internal employee development and career programs. These are the companies most likely to be able to retain the traditional model of organizational careers, so it's likely that the changes we measured would be greater in smaller corporations. We chose the baseline year 1980 because it immediately preceded the watershed recession of 1981. We wanted to see whether the early 1980s represented a major transition point in executive careers, as conventional wisdom holds. We used 2001 for comparison because when we began the project (in 2003), 2001 offered the most recent reliable data.

We examined each company's top ten executives— the ones who truly directed its strategic decisions. In the many cases where the tenth executive was one of several with the same title, we included all the people with that title. For more detail on our methodology and outcomes, please see www.nber.org/papers/w10507.

Graduates of Elite Schools Lose Ground

THE TOP EXECUTIVES OF powerful companies once shared the common bond of elite education. Increasingly, graduates of non–Ivy League institutions have worked their way up the corporate ranks. Between 1980 and 2001, the percentage of *Fortune* 100 top executives with Ivy League undergraduate degrees fell by four points (nearly 30%), while the proportion from public schools increased by 16 points (50%). This change in educational background may reflect a difference in the characteristics of the entry-level hires in each period. Although the pool of four-year-college graduates from which these corporations typically hire did not shift toward public institutions over this period, a greater proportion of the companies' new hires may have come from public schools. The change in educational background may also reflect a change in the attributes of those who were promoted after being hired—Ivy League graduates may have had a much higher rate of promotion in the earlier period. It is impossible to tease out the answer from these data, but it is reasonable to conclude that the erosion in the importance of an elite alma mater and the shift toward public institutions were due to changes in corporate practices, not demographics.

The results for second degrees suggest an even greater change. There is something of an increase in the proportion of second degrees, principally MBAs and law degrees, among these executives by 2001, and the percentage of Ivy postgraduate degrees declined more sharply than the percentage of Ivy undergraduate degrees. It's unclear whether this means corporations were becoming less elitist and more open to students from all levels of society. A possible explanation is simply that the Ivy League produced a smaller fraction of graduates over time, especially in the exploding area of professional degrees.

Originally published in January 2005
Reprint R0501B

Winning the Talent War for Women

Sometimes It Takes a Revolution

DOUGLAS M. MCCRACKEN

Executive Summary

IN 1991, Deloitte & Touche got a wake-up call about its efforts to retain women professionals. While it was recruiting almost as many women as men, the company had a much higher turnover rate for women.

Many in the firm thought Deloitte was doing everything it could to retain talented women, but when they looked harder, they found otherwise. Most women weren't leaving to raise families; they were leaving after having weighed their unpromising career options in Deloitte's male-dominated culture. CEO Mike Cook led the way in making a business case—not a moral or emotional one—for change. Next, the company held mandatory, two-day, intensive workshops for its 5,000 U.S. managers. Case vignettes and discussions brought out subtle gender-based assumptions about careers and aspirations that had discouraged high-performing women from staying.

The workshops were instrumental in convincing a critical mass of partners to join the effort, and the firm began to monitor the progress of women to ensure they received their share of mentoring and premier assignments. Executive compensation became linked to how successfully units implemented a flexible menu of goals. And other policies promoted a better balance between work and life for both men and women. Finally, an external advisory council kept the firm's feet to the fire.

Deloitte's gender gap in turnover has now nearly vanished, and the number of women partners and directors is the highest among the Big Five. These cultural changes weren't easy, but they've enabled Deloitte to grow faster than any of its competitors.

Nine years ago, we came to grips with the fact that women at Deloitte were on the march—out the door. In 1991, only four of our 50 candidates for partner were women, even though Deloitte & Touche—America's third largest accounting, tax, and consulting firm at the time—had been heavily recruiting women from colleges and business schools since 1980. Not only that. We also found that women were leaving the firm at a significantly greater rate than men.

To be frank, many of the firm's senior partners, including myself, didn't actually see the exodus of women as a problem, or at least, it wasn't *our* problem. We assumed that women were leaving to have children and stay home. If there was a problem at all, it was society's or the women's, not Deloitte's. In fact, most senior partners firmly believed we were doing everything possible to retain women. We prided ourselves on our open, collegial, performance-based work environment.

How wrong we were, and how far we've come.

Over the next few years, we analyzed why women were leaving and worked to stop the outflow. At first, the program was largely our CEO's idea; unlike many of us, he saw women's leaving as a serious business matter that the firm could and should fix.

These days, you'd be hard-pressed to find partners within the firm who disagree. It took a cultural revolution, but Deloitte now has a radically different approach to retaining talented women. Based on six principles, it is an approach that other companies might well consider, for its results speak for themselves.

Today 14% of our partners and directors are women. While we aren't yet where we want to be, this percentage is up from 5% in 1991 and the highest in the Big Five. The number of women managing partners has increased dramatically, and we've eliminated the gender gap in our turnover: women now stay on at about the same rate as men each year. The firm's annual turnover rate as a whole fell from around 25% in the early 1990s to 18% in 1999, despite an intensifying war for talent. Besides saving us $250 million in hiring and training costs, lower turnover has enabled Deloitte to grow faster than any other large professional services firm in the past several years.

A Two-Stage Process

Deloitte's Initiative for the Retention and Advancement of Women grew out of a 1992 task force chaired by Mike Cook, then CEO of Deloitte & Touche. A number of women partners initially wanted nothing to do with the effort because it implied affirmative action. But Cook, along with a handful of partners—women and men— insisted that high turnover for women was a problem of the utmost urgency. In professional services firms, they argued, the "product" is talent, billed to the client by the hour; and so much of our firm's product was leaving at an alarming rate. Cook made sure that both women and men were part of the task force and that it represented a broad range of views, including outright skepticism.

Once in place, the task force didn't immediately launch a slew of new organizational policies aimed at outlawing bad behavior. Instead, it approached the problem methodically, just as we would approach a consulting assignment. Thus, it first investigated the problem and gathered the data necessary to make a business case—not a moral or emotional one—for change. Then it prepared the groundwork for change by holding a series of intensive, two-day workshops for all of our management professionals. These sessions were designed to bring to the surface the gender-based assumptions about careers and aspirations that had discouraged high-performing women from staying.

Only then did the firm announce a series of policies aimed at keeping women. A major component of these policies was to first get all the firm's offices to monitor the progress of their women professionals. The head of every office received the message that the CEO and other managing partners were watching, and in turn, women started getting their share of premier client assignments and informal mentoring. Other policies, designed to promote more balance between work and life for women and men, also helped. These efforts have opened up our work environment and our culture in ways we never expected.

Preparing the Way for Change

Along the way, we've learned a series of lessons. Other companies, with different traditions and operating environments, may well follow other paths to achieve equitable treatment of men and women. But we think our lessons will apply to a great many organizations.

MAKE SURE SENIOR MANAGEMENT IS FRONT AND CENTER

Despite its name, the Women's Initiative was always driven by the managing partners—it never became an "HR thing" foisted on the firm. Like other organizations, we were used to having new personnel programs every so often, just one more thing added to an already full plate. I'm sure most of our partners felt initially that the focus on women was the latest "program of the year"; we would try our best and then move on to something else. But from the start, senior management signaled that the initiative would be led by the partners. Cook named Ellen Gabriel, a star partner, as the first leader of the initiative.

Cook's own leadership involved no small investment and risk. In a firm like ours, where the partners are also owners, leadership is not top-down. He took charge of the effort personally and visibly, and with every step, we all got the sense that change was a high priority for him. In Cook's case, a reputation for toughness helped to give this initiative credibility.

MAKE AN AIRTIGHT BUSINESS CASE FOR CULTURAL CHANGE

The task force prepared the firm for change by laying a foundation of data, including personal stories. Deloitte was doing a great job of hiring high-performing women; in fact, women often earned higher performance ratings than men in their first years with the firm. Yet the percentage of women decreased with each step up the career ladder, in all practices and regions, and many women left the firm just when they were expected to receive promotions. Interviews with current and former women professionals explained why. Most weren't leaving to raise families; they had weighed their options in Deloitte's male-dominated culture and found them wanting. Many of them, dissatisfied with a culture they perceived as endemic to professional services firms, switched professions. And all of them together represented a major lost opportunity for the firm.

These facts made for a sobering report to the senior partners on the firm's management committee in 1993. As Cook summarized, "Half of our hires are now women, and almost all of them have left before becoming partner candidates. We know that in order to get enough partners to grow the business, we're going to have to go deeper and deeper into the pool of new hires. Are you willing to have more and more of your partners taken from lower and lower in the talent pool? *And* let the high-performing women go elsewhere in the marketplace?"

LET THE WORLD WATCH YOU

With the endorsement of the management committee, the firm moved forward. It held a press conference to launch the Women's Initiative, but it also went further and named an external advisory council. Chaired by Lynn Martin, former U.S. secretary of labor, the council comprised business leaders with expertise in the area of women in the workplace. Besides reviewing the initiative's progress, the council brought visibility to the effort. As the task force realized, going public would put healthy pressure on the partners to commit to change and deliver results. And that's what happened, particularly with slow-moving offices in the organization. Local managers received prodding comments from their associates like, "I read in the *Wall Street Journal* that we're doing this major initiative, but I don't see big change in our office."

The council has held the firm's feet to the fire in a variety of ways: an annual report on the initiative; periodic voice-mail updates from Lynn Martin to the entire firm; and full-day meetings of the council with the firm's senior executives. The council defines the challenges we still face, and it lets senior management know they're not off the hook.

Along with helping the task force think about gender, the council has opened the firm's eyes to broader issues. In 1994, the council was meeting with a group of eight professionals—four men and four women—identified by their managers as rising stars at Deloitte. At the end of the meeting, one member of the council asked, almost as an afterthought, "How many of you want to be partners next time we see you?" Only one of the eight said yes. Stunned, the council asked for an explanation.

They were surprised to find that young men in the firm didn't want what older men wanted; they weren't trying to buy good enough lifestyles so that their wives didn't have to work. At the time, the average partner at Deloitte was making $350,000 and working 80 hours a week, but these young people—men and women both— would've been happy working 60 hours a week for $250,000. They believed they were good enough, and they weren't willing to give up their families and outside lives for another $100,000. One council member recalls, "When we asked if they wanted to be partners, we thought they were going to salute and thank us and hope we put nice letters in their files. Instead they looked at us and said, 'Perhaps.' "

BEGIN WITH DIALOGUE AS THE PLATFORM FOR CHANGE

The task force had found that women at Deloitte perceived they had fewer career opportunities than men, but no one could point to any specific policies as the culprits. We had to tackle our underlying culture to fix the problem. Accordingly, the firm held special two-day workshops designed to explore issues of gender in the workplace. We needed to begin a dialogue: in our view, the key to creating cultural change in the firm was to turn taboo subjects at work into acceptable topics of discussion.

During 1992 and 1993, nearly every management professional at Deloitte & Touche—5,000 people, including the board of directors, the management committee, and the managing partners of all of our U.S. offices— attended the workshop in groups of 24. Cook personally monitored attendance; as one partner puts it, "Resistance was futile." Many harbored doubts. I myself saw it as just one more thing to do, and I had always been skeptical of HR-type programs. I'm sure I wasn't the only partner calculating in my head the lost revenue represented by two days' worth of billable hours, multiplied by 5,000—not to mention the $8 million cost of the workshops themselves.

I was dead wrong. The workshops were a turning point, a pivotal event in the life of the firm. Through discussions, videos, and case studies, we began to take a hard look at how gender attitudes affected the environment at Deloitte. It wasn't enough to hear the problems in the abstract; we had to see them face to face. Sitting across a table from a respected colleague and hearing her say, "Why did you make that assumption about women? It's just not true," I, like many others, began to change.

The lightbulbs went on for different partners at different times. Many of us had little exposure to dual-career families but did have highly educated daughters entering the workforce. A woman partner would say to a male counterpart, "Sarah's graduating from college. Would you want her to work for a company that has lower expectations for women?" Suddenly he'd get it.

Case studies were useful for bringing out and examining subtle differences in expectations. Drawing on scripts provided by outside facilitators, people in the workshops would break into groups, discuss cases, and share solutions with the full group. A typical scenario would have partners evaluating two promising young professionals, a woman and a man with identical skills. Of the woman, a partner would say, "She's really good, she gives 100%. But I just don't see her interacting with a CFO. She's not as polished as some. Her presentation skills could be stronger." The conversation about the man would vary slightly, but significantly: "He's good. He and I are going to take a CFO golfing next week. I know he can grow into it; he has tremendous potential." Beginning with these subtle variations in language, careers could go in very different directions. A woman was found a bit wanting, and we (male partners) couldn't see how she would get to the next level. As one woman summed up, "Women get evaluated on their performance; men get evaluated on their potential."

Another scenario had two members of a team arriving late for an early-morning meeting. Both were single parents, one a father and one a mother. The team joked about and then forgot the man's tardiness but assumed the woman was having child-care problems. After the meeting, the team leader, a woman, suggested that she think seriously about her priorities.

Senarios like these lent realism to the workshop discussions, and hard-hitting dialogue often ensued. One partner was jolted into thinking about an outing he was going to attend, an annual "guys' weekend" with partners from the Atlanta office and many of their clients. It was very popular, and there were never any women. It hadn't occurred to him to ask why. He figured "no woman would want to go to a golf outing where you smoke cigars and drink beer and tell lies." But the women in the session were quick to say that by not being there, they were frozen out of informal networks where important information was shared and a sense of belonging built. Today women are routinely included in such outings.

Work assignments got a lot of attention in the workshops. Everyone knew that high-profile, high-revenue assignments were the key to advancement in the firm. Careers were made on big clients; you grew up on the Microsoft engagement, the Chrysler engagement. But the process of assigning these plum accounts was largely unexamined. Too often, women were passed over for certain assignments because male partners made assumptions about what they wanted: "I wouldn't put her on that kind of company because it's a tough manufacturing environment," or "That client is difficult to deal with."

Even more common, "Travel puts too much pressure on women," or "Her husband won't go along with relocating." Usually we weren't even conscious of making such assumptions, but the workshops brought them front and center.

The workshops also highlighted one of the worst aspects of these hidden assumptions: they were self-fulfilling. Say a partner gets a big new client and asks the assignment director to put together a team, adding, "Continuity is very important on this engagement." The assignment director knows that women turn over more rapidly than men and has the numbers to prove it. So the thinking goes, "If I put a woman on this account, the partner will be all over me—and that's who evaluates me." In the end, John gets to work on the big account and Jane works "somewhere else." After a while, Jane says, "I'm not going anywhere here. I'm never going to get the big opportunities," so she leaves. And the assignment director says, "I knew it."

The task force realized the workshops were risky; the firm was opening a can of worms and couldn't control the results. Indeed, a few of the workshops flopped, disintegrating into a painful mixture of bitterness and skepticism. Some people dismissed the experience as a waste of time. But ultimately the workshops converted a critical mass of Deloitte's leaders. The message was out: don't make assumptions about what women do or don't want. Ask them.

Putting the New Attitudes to Work

The workshops generated momentum, but the dialogue had to be followed with concrete operational steps if we were going to bring about real change. The task force had clear expectations: more of our qualified women should be promoted, and the turnover rate for women should fall. But the firm had to be careful not to set quotas or seem to give women all the plum assignments. The key was to send a clear, powerful message for change while still giving heads of local offices some discretion.

USE A FLEXIBLE SYSTEM OF ACCOUNTABILITY

Since the fastest way to change behaviors is to measure them, the task force started by simply asking for numbers. Beginning in 1993, in the midst of the workshops, local offices were asked to conduct annual reviews to determine if the top-rated women were receiving their proportionate share of the best assignments. Some offices resisted, questioning the usefulness of this time-consuming exercise or fearing that the initiative would lead to quotas. However, a few pointed phone calls from the CEO prodded the laggards. The reviews confirmed our suspicions: women tended to be assigned to projects in nonprofit, health care, and retail—segments that generally lacked large global accounts—while men received most of the assignments in manufacturing, financial services, and highly visible areas like mergers and acquisitions.

The reviews had their intended effect. Like many other managing partners, I began routinely discussing assignment decisions with the partners in charge of project staffing to make sure women had opportunities for key engagements. Most offices began tracking the activities of their high-performing women on a quarterly basis. To complement the connections that men naturally

made with one another, we began hosting regular networking events for women—for example, panel discussions where women partners discussed their careers and
leadership roles, followed by networking receptions. We
also started formal career planning for women partners
and senior managers. This planning proved so helpful
that women suggested men also be included, thus giving
rise to Deloitte Consulting's current Partner Development Program.

Only after the operational changes had percolated
through the organization did the task force introduce
clear accountability for the changes that were being
made. It offered offices a list of goals derived from the
Women's Initiative—such as a recruiting hit rate or a
reduction in the gender gap in turnover—yet left it up to
the offices to pick the goals best suited for their particular situations. Office heads started including their
choices among the objectives that drove their year-end
evaluations and compensation. And the firm made sure
that results on turnover, promotion, and other key numbers for each office were circulated widely among management, feeding a healthy internal competitiveness.
Low-performing offices got calls or visits from task force
members to push for better progress. Today partners
know that they will not become leaders of this organization if they have not demonstrated their commitment to
the Women's Initiative.

It's Not Just About Women

Moving toward equality in career development was fundamental. But as people began to discuss gender issues
in workshops, meetings, and hallways, what started out

as a program for women soon began to affect our overall corporate culture.

PROMOTE WORK-LIFE BALANCE FOR MEN AND WOMEN

We discovered that work-life balance was important to everyone. On paper, we had always allowed temporary, flexible work arrangements, but people believed (rightly, at the time) that working fewer hours could doom an otherwise promising career. In 1993, only a few hundred people were taking advantage of the policy. So now we said that opting for flexible work wouldn't hinder advancement in the firm, though it might stretch out the time required for promotion. Use of these arrangements became one more benchmark of an office's progress with the initiative. And when a woman was admitted to the partnership in 1995 while on a flexible work arrangement, people really began to get the message. By 1999 more than 30 people on flexible work arrangements had made partner, and in that year, the total number of people on flexible schedules had doubled to 800.

We also reexamined the schedule that all of us work, especially within the consulting practice. A grinding travel schedule had long been an accepted part of the macho consultants' culture. Typically, a consultant was away from home five days a week, for up to 18 months at a time. In 1996, we started a new schedule, dubbed the 3-4-5 program. Consultants working on out-of-town projects were to be away from home three nights a week, at the client site four days a week, and in their local Deloitte offices on the fifth day.

The 3-4-5 schedule hasn't been feasible on all projects—for example, those with tight deadlines like Y2K-driven system implementations. In fact, many of us were concerned initially that the program would compromise client service. But most clients embraced our new program. It turned out that employees from the client's regional offices were exhausted, too, by traveling to meet Deloitte's team at their home offices all week long. One day each week without the Deloitte consultants at their sites was a relief, not an inconvenience! By breaking the collective silence about the personal price everyone was paying, we made everyone happier. We now expect the vast majority of all projects to conform to 3-4-5.

As a result of these and other changes, we've transformed our culture into one in which people are comfortable talking about aspects of their personal lives, going well beyond client assignments and career development. Teams are getting requests like "I want to talk to my kids every night at 7:00 for half an hour," or "I'd really like to go to the gym in the morning, so can we start our meetings at 8:30 instead of 7:30?" This more open environment not only helps us keep our rising stars but also makes us more creative in a variety of areas.

A New Outlook

The changes at Deloitte are by no means complete. For many years, women have made up one-third to one-half of Deloitte's recruits, so we need to make sure the percentage of women partners and directors rises well above 14%. And we face new challenges. Now that more women are becoming partners, how can we make sure they continue to develop and advance into positions of leadership? In an increasingly global firm, how can we extend the values of the initiative while respecting local cultural differences?

Still, we have transformed our work environment, even in the smallest details. When a visiting speaker—even a client—cracks a joke at women's expense, none of us laughs, not even politely. One partner turned down an invitation to join a premier lunch club in Manhattan when he learned it excluded women. And we've opened our eyes to differences in style that go beyond gender to include culture. For example, on a recent client engagement, the project manager described an Asian consultant on his team as "shy" and therefore not ready to take on more responsibility. But another partner pushed the project manager for details and suggested that consultants could still be successful even if they didn't "command a room" or raise their voices when speaking in meetings.

We've not only narrowed the gender gap; we've narrowed the gap between who we think we are and who we truly are. Now when I say ours is a meritocracy, I'm speaking about men and women. It's not easy to manage a diverse group of people; we have to be creative and flexible in developing coaching and mentoring capabilities. Although the Women's Initiative has made managing more complicated, the benefits are substantial: greater creativity, faster growth, and far greater performance for our clients.

Lessons from Deloitte's Women's Initiative

Make sure senior management is front and center.

To overcome the resistance of partners, the CEO actively led the Women's Initiative. He put his own reputation on the line.

Make an airtight business case for cultural change.

Emotional appeals weren't going to be enough. We had to document the business imperative for change before we could justify the investment and effort that the initiative would require.

Let the world watch you.

We appointed an external advisory council and told the press about our plans. They wouldn't let the initiative be another "program of the year" that led nowhere.

Begin with dialogue as the platform for change.

We required everyone to attend intensive workshops to reveal and examine gender-based assumptions in mentoring and client assignments.

Use a flexible system of accountability.

We first required local offices to measure their efforts with women professionals. Next, we worked with the office heads to select their focus areas for change under the initiative.

Promote work-life balance for men and women.

Policies for flexible work arrangements and lighter travel schedules not only eased the strain on busy professionals but also helped open our corporate culture.

**Originally published in November–December 2000
Reprint R00611**

A Modest Manifesto For Shattering the Glass Ceiling

DEBRA E. MEYERSON AND
JOYCE K. FLETCHER

Executive Summary

ALTHOUGH WOMEN HAVE MADE enormous gains in
the business world—they hold seats on corporate boards
and run major companies—they still comprise only 10%
of senior managers in *Fortune* 500 companies. What
will it take to shatter the glass ceiling? According to
Debra Meyerson and Joyce Fletcher, it's not a revolution
but a strategy of small wins—a series of incremental
changes aimed at the subtle discriminatory forces that still
reside in organizations.

It used to be easy to spot gender discrimination in the
corporate world, but today overt displays are rare.
Instead, discrimination against women lingers in common
work practices and cultural norms that appear unbiased.
Consider how managers have tried to rout gender discrimination in the past. Some tried to assimilate women
into the workplace by teaching them to act like men.

Others accommodated women through special policies and benefits. Still others celebrated women's differences by giving them tasks for which they are "well suited." But each of those approaches proffers solutions for the symptoms, not the sources, of gender inequity.

Gender bias, the authors say, will be undone only by a persistent campaign of incremental changes that discover and destroy the deeply embedded roots of discrimination. Because each organization is unique, its expressions of gender inequity are, too. Drawing on examples from companies that have used the small-wins approach, the authors advise readers on how they can make small wins at their own organizations. They explain why small wins will be driven by men and women together, because both will ultimately benefit from a world where gender is irrelevant to the way work is designed and distributed.

THE NEW MILLENNIUM PROVIDES an occasion to celebrate the remarkable progress made by women. That women now hold seats on corporate boards, run major companies, and are regularly featured on the covers of business magazines as prominent leaders and power brokers would have been unimaginable even a half century ago.

But the truth is, women at the highest levels of business are still rare. They comprise only 10%of senior managers in *Fortune* 500 companies; less than 4% of the uppermost ranks of CEO, president, executive vice president, and COO; and less than 3% of top corporate earners.[1] Statistics also suggest that as women approach the top of the corporate ladder, many jump off, frustrated or disillusioned with the business world. Clearly, there have been gains, but as we enter the year 2000, the glass ceiling remains. What will it take to finally shatter it?

Not a revolution. Not this time. In 1962, 1977, and even 1985, the women's movement used radical rhetoric and legal action to drive out overt discrimination, but most of the barriers that persist today are insidious—a revolution couldn't find them to blast away. Rather, gender discrimination now is so deeply embedded in organizational life as to be virtually indiscernible. Even the women who feel its impact are often hard-pressed to know what hit them.

That is why we believe that the glass ceiling will be shattered in the new millennium only through a strategy that uses *small wins*[2]—incremental changes aimed at biases so entrenched in the system that they're not even noticed until they're gone. Our research shows that the small-wins strategy is a powerful way of chipping away the barriers that hold women back without sparking the kind of sound and fury that scares people into resistance. And because the small-wins strategy creates change through diagnosis, dialogue, and experimentation, it usually improves overall efficiency and performance. The strategy benefits not just women but also men and the organization as a whole.

The Problem with No Name

Time was, it was easy to spot gender discrimination in the corporate world. A respected female executive would lose a promotion to a male colleague with less experience, for instance, or a talented female manager would find herself demoted after her maternity leave. Today such blatant cases are rare; they've been wiped out by laws and by organizations' increased awareness that they have nothing to gain, and much to lose, by keeping women out of positions of authority.

That doesn't mean, however, that gender inequity has vanished. It has just gone underground. Today discrimination against women lingers in a plethora of work practices and cultural norms that only appear unbiased. They are common and mundane—and woven into the fabric of an organization's status quo—which is why most people don't notice them, let alone question them. But they create a subtle pattern of *systemic* disadvantage, which blocks all but a few women from career advancement.

For an example of this modern-day gender inequity, take the case of a global retail company based in Europe that couldn't figure out why it had so few women in senior positions and such high turnover among women in its middle-manager ranks. The problem was particularly vexing because the company's executives publicly touted their respect for women and insisted they wanted the company to be "a great place for women to work."

Despite its size, the company had a strong entrepreneurial culture. Rules and authority were informal; people were as casual about their schedules as they were about the dress code. Meetings were routinely canceled and regularly ran late. Deadlines were ignored because they constantly shifted, and new initiatives arose so frequently that people thought nothing of interrupting one another or declaring crises that demanded immediate attention.

The company's cultural norms grew from its manner of conducting business. For instance, managers were expected to be available at all times to attend delayed or emergency meetings. And these meetings themselves followed certain norms. Because roles and authority at the company were ambiguous, people felt free to make suggestions—even decisions—about any area of the company that interested them. A manager in charge of window displays, for example, might very well recommend a change in merchandising, or vice versa. To prevent changes in their own area from being made without their input, managers scrambled to attend as many meetings as possible. They had to in order to protect their turf.

The company's norms made it extraordinarily difficult for everyone—women and men—to work effectively. But they were particularly pernicious for women for two reasons. First, women typically bear a disproportionate amount of responsibility for home and family and thus have more demands on their time outside the office. Women who worked set hours—even if they spanned ten hours a day—ended up missing essential conversations and important plans for new products. Their circumscribed schedules also made them appear less committed than their male counterparts. In most instances, that was not the case, but the way the company operated day to day—its very system—made it impossible to prove otherwise.

The meetings themselves were run in a way that put women in a double bind. People often had to speak up to defend their turf, but when women did so, they were vilified. They were labeled "control freaks"; men acting the same way were called "passionate." As one female executive told us, "If you stick your neck out, you're dead."

A major investment firm provides another example of how invisible—even unintentional—gender discrimination thrives in today's companies. The firm sincerely wanted to increase the number of women it was hiring from business schools. It reasoned it would be able to hire more women if it screened more women, so it increased the number of women interviewed during recruiting visits to business school campuses. The change, however, had no impact. Why? Because, the 30 minutes allotted for each interview—the standard practice at most business schools—was not long enough for middle-aged male managers, who were conducting the vast majority of the interviews, to connect with young female candidates sufficiently to see beyond their directly relevant technical abilities. Therefore, most women were disqualified from the running. They hadn't had enough time to impress their interviewer.

The Roots of Inequity

The barriers to women's advancement in organizations today have a relatively straightforward cause. Most organizations have been created by and for men and are based on male experiences. Even though women have entered the workforce in droves in the past generation, and it is generally agreed that they add enormous value, organizational definitions of competence and leadership are still predicated on traits stereotypically associated with men: tough, aggressive, decisive. And even though many households today have working fathers and mothers, most organizations act as if the historical division of household labor still holds—with women primarily responsible for matters of the hearth. Outdated or not, those realities drive organizational life. Therefore, the global retail company was able to develop a practice of late and last-minute meetings because most men can be available 15 hours a day. The investment firm developed a practice of screening out women candidates because men, who were doing most of the interviewing, *naturally* bond with other men. In other words, organizational practices mirror societal norms.

That the "problem with no name" arises from a male-based culture does not mean that men are to blame. In fact, our perspective on gender discrimination does not presume intent, and it certainly does not assume that all men benefit from the way work is currently organized. Lots of companies run by men are working hard to create a fair environment for both sexes. And many men do not embrace the traditional division of labor; some men surely wish the conventions of a *Father Knows Best* world would vanish.

Men, then, are not to blame for the pervasive gender inequity in organizations today—but neither are women. And yet our research shows that ever since gender inequity came onto the scene as one of business's big problems, women have blamed themselves. That feeling has been reinforced by managers who have tried to solve the problem by fixing women. Indeed, over the past 30-odd years, organizations have used three approaches to rout gender discrimination, each one implying that women are somehow to blame because they "just don't fit in."

Tall People in a Short World

To describe the three approaches, we like to use a metaphor that replaces gender with height. Imagine, therefore, a world made by and for short people. In this world, everyone in power is under five-foot-five, and the most powerful are rarely taller than five-foot-three. Now imagine that after years of discrimination, tall people finally call for change—and short people agree that the current world is unfair and amends should be made.

Short people first try to right things by teaching tall people to act like short people—to minimize their differences by stooping to fit in the doorways, for example, or by hunching over to fit in the small chairs in the conference room. Once tall people learn these behaviors, short people insist, they will fit right in.

Some short people take another approach to routing discrimination: they make their world more accommodating to tall people by fixing some of the structural barriers that get in their way. They build six-foot-high doors in the back of the building and purchase desks that don't knock tall people's knees. They even go so far as to create some less demanding career paths—tall-people tracks— for those who are unwilling or unable to put up with the many realities of the short world that just can't be changed.

Other short people take a third approach: they celebrate the differences of their tall associates. Tall people stand out in a crowd, short people say, and they can reach things on high shelves. Let's recognize the worth of those skills and put them to good use! And so the short people "create equity" by putting tall people in jobs where their height is an advantage, like working in a warehouse or designing brand extensions targeted to tall people.

Those three approaches should sound familiar to anyone who has been involved in the many gender initiatives proliferating in the corporate world. Companies that take the first approach encourage women to assimilate—to adopt more masculine attributes and learn the "games their mothers never taught them." Thus, HR departments train women in assertive leadership, decision making, and even golf. Male colleagues take women to their lunch clubs, coach them on speaking up more in meetings, and suggest they take "tough guy" assignments in factories or abroad.

Companies that take the second approach accommodate the unique needs and situations of women. Many

offer formal mentoring programs to compensate for
women's exclusion from informal networks. Others add
alternative career tracks or an extra year on the tenure
clock to help women in their childbearing years. Still others offer extended maternity leave, flexible work arrangements, even rooms for nursing infants.

In the third approach, companies forgo assimilation
and accommodation and instead emphasize the differences that women bring to the workplace. They institute
sensitivity training to help male managers appreciate
traditionally "feminine" activities or styles, such as lis-
tening and collaborating. And they eagerly put women's
assumed differences to work by channeling them into
jobs where they market products to women or head up
HR initiatives.

All of these approaches have helped advance women's
equity in the corporate world. But by now they have gone
about as far as they can. Why? Because they proffer solutions that deal with the *symptoms* of gender inequity
rather than the sources of inequity itself. Take the first
approach. While many female executives can now play
golf and have used relationships formed on the fairways
to move into positions of greater power, these new skills
will never eradicate the deeply entrenched, systemic factors within corporations that hold many women back.

The same is true of the second approach of accommodation through special policies and benefits. It gives
women stilts to play on an uneven playing field, but it
doesn't flatten out the field itself. So, for example, mentoring programs may help women meet key people in a company's hierarchy, but they don't change the fact that
informal networks, to which few women are privy, determine who really gets resources, information, and opportunities. Launching family-friendly programs doesn't
challenge the belief that balancing home and work is

fundamentally a woman's problem. And adding time to a tenure clock or providing alternative career tracks does little to change the expectation that truly committed employees put work first—they need no accommodation.

The limits of the third approach are also clear. Telling people to "value differences" doesn't mean they will. That is why so many women who are encouraged to use "feminine" skills and styles find their efforts valued only in the most marginal sense. For example, women are applauded for holding teams together and are even told, "we couldn't have succeeded without you," but when promotions and rewards are distributed, they are awarded to the "rugged individuals" who assertively promoted their own ideas or came up with a onetime technical fix. Ultimately, the celebration approach may actually channel women into dead-end jobs and reinforce unhelpful stereotypes.

A Fourth Approach: Linking Equity and Effectiveness

Since 1992, we have helped organizations implement a fourth approach to eradicating gender inequity. This approach starts with the premise—to continue the metaphor—that the world of short people cannot be repaired with piecemeal fixes aimed at how tall people act and what work they do. Because the short world has been in the making for hundreds, if not thousands, of years, its assumptions and practices—such as job descriptions that conflate the physical characteristics of short people with the requirements of the job—will not be undone by assimilation or accommodation or even celebration. It will be undone by a persistent campaign of incremental changes that discover and destroy the deeply embedded roots of discrimination. These changes will be driven by short and tall people together—because both will ultimately benefit from a world where height is irrelevant to the way work is designed and distributed.

Returning to the real world of men and women, the fourth approach starts with the belief that gender inequity is rooted in our cultural patterns and therefore in our organizational systems. Although its goals are revolutionary, it doesn't advocate revolution. Instead, it emphasizes that existing systems can be reinvented by altering the raw materials of organizing—concrete, everyday practices in which biases are expressed.

The fourth approach begins when someone, somewhere in the organization realizes that the business is grappling with a gender inequity problem. Usually, the problem makes itself known through several traditional indicators. For example, recruiting efforts fail to get women to join the company in meaningful numbers; many women are stalled just before they reach leadership positions or are not rising at the same rate as their male colleagues; women tend to hold low-visibility jobs or jobs in classic "women's" departments, such as HR; senior women are waiting longer or opting to have fewer (or no) children; women have fewer resources to accomplish comparable tasks; women's pay and pay raises are not on par with men's; and women are leaving the organization at above average rates.

After recognizing that there is a problem, the next step is diagnosis. (For a description of the diagnosis stage of the small-wins strategy, see "How to Begin Small Wins" at the end of this article.) Then people must get together to talk about the work culture and determine which everyday practices are undermining effectiveness. Next, experimentation begins. Managers can launch a small initiative—or several at one time—to try to eradicate the practices that produce inequity and replace them with practices that work better for everyone. Often the experiment works—and more quickly than people would suspect. Sometimes it fixes only the symptom and loses its link to the underlying cause. When that happens, other incremental changes must be tried before a real win occurs.

Small wins are not formulaic. Each organization is unique, and its expressions of gender inequity are, too. Consider, then, how the following companies used incremental change to bring about systemic change.

Let's begin with the European retail company that was having trouble keeping its women employees. When the problem finally became impossible to ignore, the president invited us to help the organization understand what was going on. The answer wasn't immediately obvious, of course, but as we began talking to people, it became clear that it had something to do with the lack of clarity and discipline around time. Then the question was raised, Did that lack of clarity affect men and women differently? The answer was a resounding yes.

After discussing and testing the idea further, executives started using the phrase "unbounded time" to refer to meeting overruns, last-minute schedule changes, and tardiness. The term struck a chord; it quickly circulated throughout the company and sparked widespread conversation about how meeting overload and lax scheduling damaged everyone's productivity and creativity.

At that point, the president could have asked the company's female managers to become more available (assimilation). He could have mandated that all meetings take place between nine and five (accommodation). Or he could have suggested that female employees work together in projects and at times that played to their unique strengths (celebration). Instead, he and a few other senior managers quietly began to model a more disciplined use of time, and even discouraged people who suggested last-minute or late-night meetings.

Soon people began to catch on, and a new narrative started to spread through the company. The phrase "unbounded time" was used more and more often when people wanted to signal that they thought others were contributing to ineffectiveness and inequity by being late or allowing meetings to run overtime. People realized that the lack of clarity and discipline in the company had negative consequences not just for people but also for the quality of work. Over a nine-month period, norms began to shift, and as new people were hired, senior managers made sure that they understood the company was "informal *and* disciplined." To this day, the concept of "unboundedness" pops up whenever people feel the organization is slipping back into norms that silently support gender inequity.

The small-wins strategy also worked at the investment firm that tried—unsuccessfully—to hire more women by increasing the number of interviews. After executives realized that their 30-minute interviewing approach was backfiring, they began to investigate their entire recruiting practice. They examined how the questions they asked candidates, their interview procedures, and even the places in which they were recruiting might be giving traditional people—that is, male MBAs—an advantage.

And so a series of small initiatives was launched. First, the firm lengthened its interviews to 45 minutes. Partners acknowledged that shorter interviews might have been forcing them to rely on first impressions, which are so often a function of perceived similarity. Although comfort level may make an interview go smoothly, it doesn't tell you if a candidate has valuable skills, ideas, and experience. Second, and perhaps more important, the firm revised its interviewing protocol. In the past, partners questioned candidates primarily about their previous "deal experience," which allowed only those who had worked on Wall Street to shine. Again, that practice favored men, as most investment bank associates are men. In their new approach, managers followed a set protocol and began asking candidates to talk about how they would contribute to the firm's mission. The interviews shifted radically in tone and substance. Instead of boasting from former Wall Street stars, they heard many nontraditional candidates—both women and men—describe a panoply of managerial skills, creative experiences, and diverse work styles. And indeed, these people are bringing new energy and talent into the firm. (As an added bonus, the following year the firm arrived at one prominent business school to find it was earning a reputation as a great place to work, making its recruiting efforts even more fruitful.)

Both the retail company and investment firm saw their equity and performance improve after implementing changes in their systems that could hardly be called radical. The same kind of success story can be told about an international scientific research institute. The institute, which produces new agricultural technologies for farmers, had a strong cultural norm of rewarding individual achievement. When a breakthrough was reached, a new product was developed, or a grant was won, individual scientists usually got the credit and rewards. The norm meant that support work by secretaries and technicians, as well as by scientists and professionals in departments like biotechnology and economics, was often ignored.

Paradoxically, top-level managers at the institute spoke enthusiastically about the value of teamwork and asserted that success was a group, not an individual, product. In fact, the organization planned to move to a team-based structure because senior managers considered it an imperative for addressing complex cross-functional challenges. But in the everyday workings of the organization, no one paid much heed to supporting contributors. The stars were individual "heroes."

The undervaluation of support work was an issue that affected many women because they were more likely to be in staff positions or scientific roles that were perceived as support disciplines. In addition, women more often took on support work because they were expected to do so or because they felt it was critical to a project's success. They connected people with one another, for instance, smoothed disagreements, facilitated teamwork, and taught employees new skills.

Many women expressed frustration with this type of work because it simply wasn't recognized or rewarded. Yet they were reluctant to stop because the costs of not doing it were clear to them. Without it, information would flow less easily, people would miss deadlines, more crises would erupt, and teams would break down. As we talked with them, women began to recognize the value of their efforts, and they gave them a name: "invisible work."

As in the European retail company, naming the problem had a striking effect. It turned out that invisible work wasn't just a problem for women. Men and women started talking about how the lack of value placed on invisible work was related to much larger systemic patterns. For example, people noted that the company tended to give sole credit for projects to the lead scientists, even when others had contributed or had helped spare the projects from major crises. People, especially women, admitted that mentors and bosses had advised them—and they had often advised one another—to avoid taking on invisible work to focus on work that would afford more recognition. Stemming from these informal discussions, a narrative about the importance of invisible work began to spread throughout the organization.

For senior managers who saw the link between invisible work and their goal of moving to a team-based structure, the challenge was to find ways to make invisible work visible—and to ensure it was valued and more widely shared by men and women. A task force on the topic proposed a new organizationwide evaluation system that would gather input from peers and direct reports—people to whom an employee's invisible work is visible. Although that step seemed insignificant to many, it was approved and launched.

Several years later, people say that the institute is a different place. The first small win—the new evaluation process—gave way to others, such as a new process to increase information flow up, down, and sideways; new criteria for team leaders that emphasize facilitation rather than direction; and new norms about tapping expertise, no matter where it resides in the hierarchy. Implicitly, these changes challenged the prevailing masculine, individualist image of competence and leadership and opened the way for alternatives more conducive to teamwork. Today both men and women say there is a stronger sense of fairness. And senior managers say that the systemic changes brought about by the small-wins strategy were central to the institute's successful move to a team-based structure.

Small Wins Can Make Big Gains

It's surprising how quickly people can come up with ideas for small wins—and how quickly they can be put into action. Take, for example, the case of the finance department at a large manufacturing company. The department had a strong norm of *overdoing* work. Whenever senior managers asked for information, the department's analysts would generate multiple scenarios complete with sophisticated graphs and charts.

The fact was, however, senior managers often only wanted an analyst's back-of-the-envelope estimates. People in the finance department even suspected as much, but there was an unspoken policy of never asking the question. The reasons? First, they worried that questions would indicate that they couldn't figure out the scope of the request themselves and hence were not competent. Second, many of the requests came in at the end of the day. Analysts feared that asking, "How much detail do you want?" might look like a way to avoid working late. To show their commitment, they felt they had to stay and give every request the full treatment.

The norm of devoting hours on end to each request hit women in the department especially hard. As women in an industry dominated by men, they felt they had to work extra hard to demonstrate their competence and commitment, especially when commitment was measured, at least in part, by time spent at work. However, the norm negatively affected men, too. The extra work, simply put, was a waste of time; it lowered productivity and dampened enthusiasm. The organization suffered: talented people avoided the department because of its reputation for overtime.

The small-wins process at this company began when we met with a group of analysts and managers in the finance department. We presented our diagnosis of the root causes of the overwork problem and asked if they could come up with small, concrete solutions to counteract it. It didn't take them long. Within an hour, the analysts had designed a one-page form that asked senior managers to describe the parameters of each request. How much detail was required? What was the desired output? The form very simply took the onus off individuals to ask taboo questions, relieving women of the fear that they might appear less than committed and allowing all analysts—not just women—to use their time more productively.

Interestingly, after only a short time, the form was dropped. Analysts reported that simply having a conversation with their managers about the company's norms and taboos changed the department's dynamics. By establishing an open dialogue, analysts could now ask clarifying questions without fearing that they were signaling incompetence or lack of commitment.

Small wins make sense even at companies that already have programs designed to combat gender inequity. Consider the case of a New York advertising agency that was particularly proud of its mentoring program aimed at developing high-potential female leaders. Although that program got women's names into the mix, the jobs that women were ultimately offered tended to be in human resource-type positions—positions women were thought to be particularly well suited for. These jobs often required a high level of skill, but their lack of rainmaking potential resulted in career disadvantages that accumulated over time.

The situation was compounded by an unspoken rule at the company of never saying no to developmental opportunities. This norm, like so many others, seems gender neutral. It appears to be a risk for both men and women to pass up opportunities, particularly those offered in the name of developing leadership potential. Yet because of the different types of opportunities offered, women stood to lose whether they said yes or no. Saying no signaled lack of commitment. But saying yes meant they would spend valuable time and energy doing a job that was unlikely to yield the same career benefits that men were deriving from the opportunities offered to them. What made the situation particularly problematic for the organization was that the HR-type jobs that women were reluctant to accept were often critical to overall functioning.

The women in the mentoring programs were the first to realize the negative impact of the company's informal policy of channeling women into these critical HR positions. So they got together to brainstorm about ways to extricate themselves from their double bind. (Like many small-wins campaigns, this one was launched with the knowledge and approval of senior management. For ideas on how to start the change process without official sanction, see "Going It Alone" at the end of this article.) The women coached one another on how to respond to the HR-type job offers in ways that would do minimal damage to their careers. For instance, they came up with the solution of accepting the job with the stipulation that senior managers assign its year-end objectives a "rainmaking equivalency quotient." The group pushed senior managers to think about the underlying assumptions of putting women in HR jobs. Did they really believe men could not manage people? If so, didn't that mean that men should be given the developmental opportunities in HR? These questions led senior managers to several revelations, which were especially important since the organization had recently decided to sell itself to potential clients as the relationship-oriented alternative to other agencies. The full effect of this small-win effort, launched recently, will likely be seen over the course of the next few years.

The Power of Small Wins

Small wins are not silver bullets; anyone familiar with real organizational change knows that there is no such thing. Rather, the reason small wins work so effectively is that they are not random efforts. They unearth and upend systemic barriers to women's progress. Consider how:

First, small wins tied to the fourth approach help organizations give a name to practices and assumptions that are so subtle they are rarely questioned, let alone seen as the root of organizational ineffectiveness. When the retail company started using the phrase "unbounded time," people began developing a shared understanding of how the lack of discipline around time affected men and women differently and how the lack of boundaries in the culture contributed to people's inability to get work accomplished. The act of naming the "problem with no name" opens up the possibility of change.

Second, small wins combine changes in behavior with changes in understanding. When a small win works— when it makes even a minor difference in systemic practices—it helps to verify a larger theory. It says that something bigger is going on.

Third, and related, small wins tie the local to the global. That is, people involved in small wins see how their efforts affect larger, systemic change, in much the same way as people taking part in small-town recycling campaigns come to understand their impact in decreasing global warming. This big-picture outlook is both energizing and self-reinforcing, and it links seemingly unrelated small wins together.

Fourth, small wins have a way of snowballing. One small change begets another, and eventually these small changes add up to a whole new system. Consider again the investment firm that revised its recruiting processes. It realized that something as simple as lengthening interview time could begin to address its recruitment problem. But if it had stopped there, it is unlikely that fundamental changes would have occurred. Recognizing why the length of an interview was an issue—how "feeling comfortable" and "fitting the mold" had been implicit selection criteria—helped the firm make additional, more substantial changes in, for instance, the questions asked. This change is encouraging the executives to look into initiatives to revise other practices, ranging from publicity to training, that also held hidden biases, not just for women but also for other underrepresented groups.

The fifth and final source of power in the small-wins approach is that it routs discrimination by fixing the organization, not the women who work for it. In that way, it frees women from feelings of self-blame and anger that can come with invisible inequity. And it removes the label of troublemaker from women who complain that something is not right. Small wins say,

"Yes, something is wrong. It is the organization itself, and when it is fixed, all will benefit."

As we enter the new millennium, we believe that it is time for new metaphors to capture the subtle, systemic forms of discrimination that still linger. It's not the ceiling that's holding women back; it's the whole structure of the organizations in which we work: the foundation, the beams, the walls, the very air. The barriers to advancement are not just above women, they are all around them. But dismantling our organizations isn't the solution. We must ferret out the hidden barriers to equity and effectiveness one by one. The fourth approach asks leaders to act as thoughtful architects and to reconstruct buildings beam by beam, room by room, rebuilding with practices that are stronger and more equitable, not just for women but for all people.

The Research: A Joint Effort

THE RESEARCH FOR THIS ARTICLE began in 1992 and is ongoing. Our work—including interviews, surveys, archival data, focus groups, and observations—has taken place at 11 organizations. They included three *Fortune* 500 companies, two international research organizations, two public agencies, a global retail organization, an investment firm, a school, and a private foundation. The goal of each project was to create the kind of small wins and learning reported in this article.

The ideas presented in this article were developed in collaboration with three colleagues: Robin Ely, an associate professor at Columbia University's School of International and Public Affairs in New York City and an affiliated faculty member at the Center for Gender in Organizations, Simmons Graduate School of Management, in Boston; Deborah Kolb, a codirector of the Center for Gender in Organizations, a professor of management at Simmons Graduate School of Management, and a senior fellow at the Program on Negotiation at Harvard Law School; and anthropologist Deborah Merrill-Sands, a codirector of the Center for Gender in Organizations and an expert in conducting research on gender in organizations.

The research in this article builds directly on the foundational work of Lotte Bailyn, the T. Wilson Professor of Management at the MIT Sloan School of Management in Cambridge, Massachusetts, and Rhona Rapoport, director of the Institute of Family and Environmental Research in London. They also collaborated on many of the projects mentioned in this article.

How to Begin Small Wins

ONCE AN ORGANIZATION DETERMINES that it has a problem—female employees won't join the company, say, or women are leaving in alarming numbers—it is time to start searching for causes. Such diagnosis involves senior managers probing an organization's practices and beliefs to uncover its deeply embedded sources of inequity. But how?

An effective first step is often one-on-one interviews with employees to uncover practices and beliefs in the company's culture—how work gets done, for instance, what activities are valued, and what the assumptions are about competence. After that, focus groups can more closely examine questionable practices. Some companies have found it useful to have women and men meet separately for these initial discussions, as long as the outcomes of these meetings are shared.

Diagnosis isn't always straightforward. After all, the group is looking for the source of a relatively invisible problem. Yet we have found a collection of questions that help keep the process on track:

- How do people in this organization accomplish their work? What, if anything, gets in the way?
- Who succeeds in this organization? Who doesn't?
- How and when do we interact with one another? Who participates? Who doesn't?
- What kinds of work and work styles are valued in this organization? What kinds are invisible?
- What is expected of leaders in this company?
- What are the norms about time in this organization?
- What aspects of individual performance are discussed the most in evaluations?
- How is competence identified during hiring and performance evaluations?

After the initial diagnosis, managers should identify cultural patterns and their consequences. For example, Which practices affect men differently than women, and why? Which ones have unintended consequences for the business? Following this analysis, change agents can discuss these patterns with different people. We call this stage "holding up the mirror," and it represents the first part of developing a new shared narrative in the organization.

The next step, of course, is designing the small wins. We have found that by this point in the process, groups usually have little trouble identifying ways to make concrete changes. It is critical, however, that the managers guiding the process keep the number and scope of initiatives relatively limited and strategically targeted. Managers and other change agents should remind the organization that a single experiment should not be seen as an end in itself. Each small win is a trial intervention and a probe for learning, intended not to overturn the system but to slowly and surely make it better.

Going It Alone

ONE OF THE MOST IMPORTANT VIRTUES of the fourth approach is that it helps people realize that they are not alone: the problems are systemic, not individual. That said, individuals or small groups may still have to "go it alone" without the support of an organizational mandate or formal change program. Although first efforts are aimed at subverting the status quo, over time they may, in fact, be embraced by the organization because they create the impetus for learning and positive change.

Individuals can adopt one of two methods. First, they can simply operate solo. They can conduct a diagnosis, identify sources of gender discrimination, and design small wins themselves. That approach is hard, as the process depends so heavily on frank discussion and testing of ideas. That is why we suggest that individuals use a second method: finding like minds to join them in the exercise. The group can be internal to the organization or it can include people from various organizations. It can include only women or it can include women and men. The point is to hear one another's stories about workplace practices and their consequences in order to discover common themes and underlying factors. Small groups can generate small wins on their own and experiment with them quietly but persistently.

So often, the "problem with no name" is experienced by women as a situation that affects them alone or worse, as a problem with them. In our executive education programs, we have seen that when women share their experiences, they recognize that many of the problems they experience as individuals are actually systemic and not unique to them or to their organization. And they realize that promoting change can benefit the organization as well as the men and women in it. That insight motivates them to work on their own and in collaboration with others to create small wins that can make a big difference.

Notes

1. Statistics on women of color are even more drastic. Although women of color make up 23% of the U.S. women's workforce, they account for only 14% of women in managerial roles. African-American women comprise only 6% of the women in managerial roles.

2. The small-wins approach to change was developed by Karl Weick. See "Small Wins: Redefining the Scale of Social Problems," *American Psychologist*, 1984.

Originally published in January-February 2000.
Reprint R00107

Work and Life

The End of the Zero-Sum Game

STEWART D. FRIEDMAN,
PERRY CHRISTENSEN, AND
JESSICA DEGROOT

Executive Summary

MOST COMPANIES VIEW WORK and personal life as competing priorities in a zero-sum game, in which a gain in one area means a loss in the other. From this traditional perspective, managers decide how their employees' work and personal lives should intersect and often view work-life programs as just so much social welfare. A new breed of managers, however, is trying a new tack, one in which managers and employees collaborate to achieve work and personal objectives to everyone's benefit.

These managers are guided by three principles. The first is to clearly inform their employees about business priorities and to encourage them to be just as clear about personal priorities. The second is to recognize and support their employees as whole people, not only acknowledging but also celebrating their roles outside the office. The third is to continually experiment with the way work gets done, looking for approaches that enhance the organization's performance and allow employees to pursue personal goals.

The managers who are acting on these principles have discovered that conflicts between work and personal priorities can actually be catalysts for identifying inefficiencies at the workplace. For example, one manager and his staff found a way to accommodate the increased workload at their 24-hour-a-day command center while granting the staff more concentrated time off.

So far, these managers have usually been applying the principles without official sanction. But as the business impact of their approach becomes better appreciated, the authors predict, more and more companies will view these leaders as heralds of change.

THE CONFLICTING DEMANDS OF work and personal life have always been with us. People have always had children and elderly parents to care for; they have always pursued hobbies and devoted time to community activities. In the past, many managers dealt with such personal needs summarily: "What you do in the office is our business. What you do outside is your own." It was assumed, too, that employees would put the company's interests first. Work versus personal life, after all, was a zero-sum game.

Have times changed? Yes and no. On one hand, striking demographic shifts, such as the increasing number of women in the workforce, have put more mothers on the job, heightening awareness of work-life issues. New economic forces, such as global competition, have also changed the landscape, creating an unprecedented need for committed employees at a time when loyalty is low in the wake of corporate downsizings. On the other hand, most executives still believe that every time an employee's personal interests "win," the organization pays the price at its bottom line. They consign work-life issues to the human resources department, where the problems are often dealt with piecemeal, through programs such as flextime and paternity leave. Such programs, however, rarely help more than a few employees strike a meaningful, sustainable balance between work and personal life because they do not permeate a company's culture or fundamentally change managers' behavior.

Under the Radar

In recent years, however, we have observed that a small but growing number of managers—many of them flying under the radar of officially sanctioned programs—approach the work-life question differently. They operate under the assumption that work and personal life are not competing priorities but complementary ones. In essence, they've adopted a win-win philosophy. And it appears they are right: in the cases we have studied, the new approach has yielded tangible payoffs both for organizations and for individual employees.

These managers are guided by three mutually reinforcing principles. First, they clarify what is important. That is, they clearly inform their employees about business priorities. And they encourage their employees to be just as clear about personal interests and concerns—to identify where work falls in the spectrum of their overall priorities in life. The objective is to hold an honest dialogue about both the business's and the individual's goals and then to construct a plan for fulfilling all of them.

Second, these managers recognize and support their employees as "whole people," open-mindedly acknowledging and even celebrating the fact that they have roles outside the office. These managers understand that skills and knowledge can be transferred from one role to another and also that boundaries—where these roles overlap and where they must be kept separate—need to be established.

Third, these managers continually experiment with the way work is done, seeking approaches that enhance the organization's performance while creating time and energy for employees' personal pursuits.

The three principles lead to a virtuous cycle. When a manager helps employees balance their work lives with the rest of their lives, they feel a stronger commitment to the organization. Their trust redoubles, and so do their loyalty and the energy they invest in work. Not surprisingly, their performance improves, and the organization benefits. Strong results allow the manager to continue practicing the principles that help employees strike this work-life balance.

In the following pages, we will explore the three principles in more detail and illustrate how managers apply them. The cases are drawn from our research into several dozen U.S.-based companies of varying sizes in a variety of industries, supplemented by over 100 interviews conducted and analyzed by our colleagues at the Wharton Work/Life Roundtable. Each case shows that striking a balance between work and personal life is not the task of the manager alone; rather, it is a process that requires a partnership between the manager and individual employees. Ultimately, all the strategies call for an honest two-sided exchange, as well as a mutual commitment to continual change.

CLARIFY WHAT'S IMPORTANT

In most organizations, employees rarely feel comfortable discussing their personal priorities. They worry that admitting a passion for singing with the local opera company, for instance, will be seen as a lack of passion for work. Such fear is not misguided. Most managers believe—or at least hope—that work is at the top of an employee's list of life priorities. For some, it is. For others, of course, work is just a means to the end of achieving other priorities. These people are often put in the uncomfortable position of having to pretend they care primarily about work-related issues that are actually of secondary importance to them.

The managers who strike a work-life balance with their people cut through the charade about priorities. They make business objectives crystal clear, and they define them in terms of outputs—in terms of results. Simultaneously, they ask employees to identify the important goals, concerns, and demands outside the office that require time and energy. One person might be responsible for his elderly mother's health care, which involves three trips to the hospital each month. Another might be in the process of qualifying for a Gold Star in figure skating. Still another may feel strongly that, at this point in her career, none of her priorities is more important than success at work.

Such a discussion of priorities can take place only in an environment of trust, and the managers who are striking a balance between work and personal life with their employees know that. They do not penalize people for putting personal concerns first or for putting them right alongside work. They do not try to persuade people to give up their extracurricular interests. Rather, they use the information about personal priorities to draw a road map toward a singular destination: business success achieved hand in hand with individual fulfillment.

The fact that these managers define business success in terms of results is key. To them, outcomes matter more than process. To that end, they give their employees specific goals but also great autonomy over how to achieve those goals. That way, the woman who is trying to receive a Gold Star in figure skating can practice in the morning when the rink is empty and rates are lower. She can arrive at work at noon, stay until 5 P.M., and then take unfinished tasks home with her to complete in the evening. To her manager, such a schedule is acceptable as long as she is producing the work her job requires.

Steve, a senior operations executive at a global bank, demonstrates the benefits of putting both business and personal priorities on the table. For many years, Steve was a classic hard-driving boss, given to starting the day with 7 A.M. breakfasts with his staff. He also expected his top people to work as late as he did—sometimes close to 10 P.M.

One of those people was a vice president named Jim. At first, Jim played by Steve's rules, "living at work," as he describes it. Then one weekend, Jim's young son fell and cut his knee. To Jim's shock and dismay, the child refused to let Jim comfort him. Indeed, he treated Jim like a stranger. The event was a turning point. Although fearful for his job, Jim approached Steve and said that he had let slip the single most important priority in his life—a close relationship with his son. He made an offer:

"Judge me by the quality of my work, not by the amount of time I spend at the office."

The request clearly disconcerted Steve, but because he valued Jim enormously, he agreed to evaluate Jim's performance based solely on his contributions to the bank's success. Both men then had to change how they got things done. They began to plan their time together more carefully. Their meetings became more focused; they cut down on the length and number of reports and memos they sent to each other and got right to the essentials in their communications. Until that point, Jim had helped Steve prepare for the 7 A.M. staff meetings in the half hour prior to them. Under the new arrangement, Jim briefed Steve the day before; soon, in fact, Jim was routinely skipping the 7 A.M. meetings, and his absence had little or no adverse impact. What's more, Jim was able to leave the office regularly at 5 P.M.

For his part, Steve found that Jim's energy and concentration at work soared. Indeed, having made his business and personal priorities explicit, Jim was able to pay unrelenting attention to key business issues while at work. As a result, his performance improved dramatically. He was rewarded with several promotions, rising quickly through the company's ranks.

In time, Jim went on to run a large credit-card business, and he is currently the chief operating officer of a major manufacturing company. Along the way, clarifying what's important has become a fundamental part of his managerial style. In fact, he is well known throughout his current organization for taking family and personal considerations into account in scheduling both his own time and his employees' time.

Steve recently retired. In his farewell address to the organization after a long and successful career, he noted that his experience with Jim was a milestone in his development as a leader. He learned, he said, the business value of allowing employees to meet personal commitments as they pursue organizational goals. An essential role of a leader is to make sure all priorities are part of the discussion of how to achieve success.

RECOGNIZE AND SUPPORT THE WHOLE PERSON

Most managers know about their employees' personal lives to some extent. They know, for instance, that one person has three children or that another is about to be married. Occasionally, they are aware of people's hobbies or community activities. This kind of incidental knowledge, however, bears little resemblance to the second principle as managers who balance issues of work and personal life practice it. Their understanding of employees is deeper and more detailed. Instead of knowing casual facts about people, and beyond learning about priorities, these managers recognize and support the full range of their people's life roles: not just mother or caretaker, but also volunteer with autistic children, aspiring concert pianist, or passionate golfer.

Why do these managers tune into their employees' roles outside the office? First, being sincerely interested in an employee's personal life creates a bond and, with it, trust—which brings organizational benefits familiar to any manager. Second, identifying the various roles helps these managers tap into the full range of their employees' talents. Third, it is necessary for individuals to understand how their roles relate to one another—where they mesh and where they need to be kept separate—to establish effective boundaries. Establishing the boundaries helps remove distractions, allowing people to be more fully focused on the task at hand. Finally, knowing about an employee's personal life is critical if a manager wants to put the first work-life principle to work, crafting a strategy to meet both business and personal goals.

Just as employees don't usually volunteer details of their personal priorities, neither do they openly offer information about their life roles. Indeed, such revelations are countercultural in most big companies today. That is why managers who adopt this principle demonstrate their commitment to it by acting as role models. They openly discuss the benefits and demands of their own roles outside work. The manager of a 15-person work group at a manufacturing company, for instance, freely discusses the challenges of her role as the head of a blended family. At home, she cares for six preteen children from her previous marriage and her husband's two previous marriages all living under one roof. Not only does she apply her experience resolving conflicts in her own family to settling differences within the work group, but she also openly admits, "Everything I know about negotiation I learned at the dinner table." The manager's honesty about her roles as a mother and stepmother invites her employees to be similarly candid about their personal roles.

Another way managers recognize and support the whole person is by valuing the knowledge and skills employees bring to the business from their lives outside work. In one company we studied, for example, a manager named José found out that one of his key sales representatives, Sally, was intensely dedicated to her alma mater, a Big Ten university. She was an active fund-raiser for the school and often used her free time to recruit local high-school students.

After receiving Sally's permission, José called the company's recruiting director. He described Sally's knowledge of and commitment to her alma mater and asked if it would be possible to get her assigned as the company's liaison in its recruiting efforts at the school. As it happened, the company had been having limited success at the school, and the recruiting director was looking for ways to both improve the company's reputation on campus and increase the number of students it was able to recruit, particularly for the sales force. The recruiting director welcomed the chance to talk with Sally, and they met soon thereafter.

The recruiting director was impressed with Sally's energy, ideas, and the relationships she had already forged with the university. He offered her the position of liaison, a task that would likely take up to 20% of her time for half the year. She would replace another sales rep—an individual without personal ties to the school—who was currently doing the job. Sally brought the liaison proposal to José who, despite the fact that it would mean that Sally would spend less time with her customers, recognized the business value of increasing the organization's ability to hire more sales reps from the university.

Why did he agree? First, he correctly anticipated that because of her feelings about the school, Sally would do a great job, and her relationship would bear fruit in the company's recruiting effort. Second, he accurately predicted that the loss of Sally's time with customers in the short term would be minimal since she was already spending some of her discretionary time on school events. Finally, José expected that Sally would be grateful for this opportunity to combine her interest in the school with her work. And she was. Sally told us that after she received the liaison position, her commitment to the company skyrocketed. As often is the case, exercising the principle of recognizing and supporting the whole person benefited not just the individual but the company as well.

CONTINUALLY EXPERIMENT WITH THE WAY WORK IS DONE

Most managers in today's rapidly changing business environment know how important it is to find ways to increase efficiency and productivity. Still, new methods and different ways of thinking about work can be daunting, if not threatening. Managers who embrace the third work-life principle, however, see experimenting with work processes as an exciting opportunity to improve the organization's performance and the lives of its people at the same time. They have discovered that conflicts between work and personal priorities can actually be catalysts for identifying work inefficiencies that might otherwise have remained hidden or intractable. That's because taking a new set of parameters into account can allow people to question ways of doing business so ingrained that no one would think to consider changing them otherwise.

These managers encourage employees to question basic assumptions, such as the common sales mantra: "Real commitment means total availability." "Does it really?" they ask. "Can we find creative ways to demonstrate total commitment to our customers without being available every waking moment?" They also encourage employees to learn, through trial and error, about new ways to organize work that might well challenge the legitimacy of existing practices.

Many work practices are legacies of outdated industrial models in which employees had to be physically present during "normal" business hours. The managers who strike a work-life balance with their employees, however, recognize that newer telecommunication tools—such as e-mail, voice mail, teleconferencing, and computer networks—can create greater flexibility in how, when, where, and with whom work is accomplished. In addition, they are willing to explore alternative arrangements like job sharing to see if they can improve organizational efficiency while freeing up employees' time.

Hallie is a manager who—by meeting both business demands and her employees' personal needs—was able to reinvent the way work was done in her organization. As the new department director at a food services company, Hallie learned that she had inherited an older employee named Sarah, an administrative assistant who was perceived to be unmotivated and cynical. Her attitude, Hallie was told by other employees, badly hurt morale. They recommended, in fact, that she fire Sarah if she could.

At Hallie's first meeting with Sarah, she learned that Sarah enjoyed working with numbers but was not permitted to do finance work because of her inexperience with computers. Hallie also learned that Sarah was caring for her mother, who was in the late stages of a terminal illness. As her mother's condition deteriorated, Sarah found she had to go to her home in the morning and again at lunch to tend to her mother's physical and household needs. In addition, Sarah also managed her own home—chores, yard work, and paying the bills.

Hallie could have heard Sarah's story and asked, "How can I rid myself of this burden?" Instead she asked, "How can we work differently, in a way that will improve the department's performance and preserve the dignity of the employee?"

Together, Hallie and Sarah explored possible answers. They were able to identify inefficiencies in the department's work processes, including those in Sarah's job. The department had been formed recently as a result of the consolidation of several different groups. Yet Sarah was maintaining separate budgeting and inventory control systems. Combining them would streamline data collection and analysis.

Knowing of Sarah's interest in finance, Hallie arranged for her to be trained on Excel, on a new Excel-based budgetary system, and in basic analytical processes, which gave her greater control over the department's finances. The change had immediate effects. Sarah now gathered more relevant data in a streamlined and logical manner, allowing managers to interpret the information faster and more intelligently. At the same time, working with numbers greatly increased Sarah's interest in her job. Her morale and performance improved markedly. And working on a computer made it easier for her to care for her mother; she could even work from home when her mother needed more attention. As a result of the change in the content and flexibility of her job, Sarah had an easier time coping with her mother's final days.

A Mutually Reinforcing System

Each of the three work-life principles might be practiced by itself, but more often they are practiced together. That's because the principles reinforce one another and, in fact, overlap to some degree. Encouraging employees to be explicit about their personal priorities, for instance, is a necessary element in recognizing and supporting an employee as a whole person. Valuing productivity over face time is a necessary element in experimenting with work processes. Both involve a manager caring more about the ends than the means. Let's look more, then, at all three principles working together.

Consider first the case of Sam, the director of a 24-hour command center at a pharmaceutical company's largest site, a plant with 8,000 employees. The 30-person center monitors more than 10,000 "hot spots" at the site, such as fire alarms; sewage lift stations; and, in particular, a hazardous manufacturing process. For example, the command center oversees several vaults that house chemicals being stored at minus 70 degrees Fahrenheit. Employees working in the vaults must wear special protective suits and are allowed to stay for only ten minutes at a time; if they stay longer, the center considers it an emergency and responds in kind. Such incidents are not uncommon and, as you might expect, work in the command center can be stressful.

Because the command center needed to be staffed around the clock, its schedule was always a challenge. Sam frequently had trouble filling the midnight to 8 A.M. slots in particular. Shifts changed 21 times each week, and exchanging information between members of incoming and outgoing shifts was cumbersome. To make matters worse, the command center was about to be handed more work. The number of hot spots under its supervision was set to increase by 50% to 15,000 within the next year and perhaps even to double to 20,000 within two years.

Sam could have seen the burgeoning workload at the command center purely as a business problem and sought an exclusively business solution. How could he fill the center's schedule, keep overtime down, and make sure information was exchanged efficiently? But Sam also realized that a heavier workload was bound to have an impact on his staff's personal lives. Financial constraints made hiring more people out of the question. The existing staff would need to work longer hours under more stressful conditions. If he ignored those facts, Sam believed, any solution he arrived at would not be sustainable. The members of his staff were not robots but whole people with rich and varied lives. Just as the business imperatives had to be accounted for, so did his people's personal needs and concerns.

Sam's first step was to call his staff together and explicitly define the command center's business goals. He talked about how the group's work was essential for the safe operation of the entire site, including the critical research and manufacturing processes. He was open about how the center's workload was sure to increase and about the fact that they could not just throw more people at the problem.

Sam had a vision of the command center as more customer focused, proactively anticipating the needs of the site. He described to the group, for example, the need to improve the way manufacturing lines were shut down for maintenance and repair. He stressed the importance of forecasting needs as far in advance as possible, rather than waiting for an emergency to galvanize everyone to action. Sam knew that to achieve his vision, everyone would have to pay more attention to feedback from the center's customers, that the staff would need more training, and that there would simply be more plain, hard work—and he told them so. At the same time, he explicitly acknowledged that the demanding workload might have a negative impact on his employees' personal lives, and he invited them to describe to him and to one another how the schedule could adversely affect them.

After that discussion, Sam opened the door for radical experimentation with the way the command center was run. He asked the staff itself to design a solution to the scheduling problem that met not only the business needs he had outlined but also their own personal requirements. As many executives who operate according to the three principles do, Sam told the employees that no solution was out of bounds as long as it produced the results they were looking for. He also told them that they did not have to solve all the center's problems at once. They could test possible plans of action, gradually learning from those experiences what would work and what would not.

Within several weeks, Sam's people had developed a comprehensive new approach to staffing the center. They would work 12-hour shifts, three days on and four days off one week, four days on and three days off the next week. Over the course of two weeks, they would work 84 hours, which worked out to four more than they had in the past. But at the same time, work schedules would be steady and predictable, and their time off more concentrated. It added up to an acceptable trade-off.

The system has now been in place for more than two years, and it has far exceeded expectations. At work, the new schedule has eliminated seven shifts, which means that information is now exchanged seven fewer times, reducing errors and oversights during shift transfers. The predictability of the schedule has reduced overtime considerably, as well as the number of personal days the employees take. In addition, the new schedule has led to a better way to train supervisors. In the past, they had been stuck in the command center whenever there was an unexpected hole in the schedule. Often they were alone on the night shift, during which they learned little and potentially compromised safety. But now they are rotated systematically into the command center in all shifts to learn the processes, systems, and safety procedures.

Much to Sam's delight, the new system has allowed the center to become the proactive, customer-focused group he had envisioned. Now that staff members work on a set schedule and aren't scrambling to fill empty spots, they can spend more time on coordination and process improvements. For example, there was a time when sales of a new drug boomed, exceeding forecasts by 300%. Unfortunately, the drug's manufacturing line was scheduled to be closed for six days of maintenance. Working with production and maintenance supervisors, the command center was able to reduce shutdown time to two days.

Finally, because the schedule has become predictable and acceptable to all, there's less strife among employees and less strife between employees and management. In short, morale is up and stress is down. Not surprisingly, productivity has improved.

At home, the new schedule has allowed employees to meet their personal needs in ways that were not possible under the old system. One person was able finally to go to school during the day to earn a master's degree. Another earned a certificate degree on her days off. Many employees have told Sam that simply feeling that their lives are predictable has allowed them to relax when they are home and plan more personal projects and events. The new schedule has been so successful from a lifestyle point of view that, somewhat ironically, it has created a high demand to work in the command center. "We are a magnet now for transfers and new hires," Sam recently observed.

We found another example of the three principles working in tandem at a global, 80,000-employee manufacturing company where senior executives were anxious to determine the best way to transfer knowledge from region to region. They decided to test a radical new approach that had two parts: a computer-based data warehouse that would allow sales representatives to collect and share sales and marketing information in real time and a territory management system that would allow each sales rep to run a fully functioning, independent operation. The success or failure of the two pilot projects would determine the company's direction for global marketing and sales.

A task force consisting of three men and three women was created to oversee and coordinate the pilot projects. It was headed by one of the women, Terry. From the outset, pressure on the group was intense; the company's leaders believed that the way the organization managed the process of learning and of transferring information was critical to its competitive success. Despite the pressure for results, Terry strongly believed that if she let business objectives nullify personal ones, the task force would fail on all counts. "To ignore people's personal issues was unrealistic," she noted. At the time, all the team members had significant personal issues: two pregnancies, three recent births, one person on a part-time schedule, another in a demanding M.B.A. program at night, and still another in the midst of a family separation.

Before the task force's first meeting, Terry met individually with each member to discuss the demands he or

she faced in the coming year and to help identify each
person's spectrum of priorities. Then, at the first group
meeting, Terry led a discussion of business objectives.
She explicitly defined what the company's leaders
expected of the team, as well as the timetables and specific tasks involved. She identified how the team's performance would be measured and what kind of results
would constitute success.

Next, Terry opened up the dialogue on personal priorities and brought in the discussion of roles. She asked a
couple of questions to get it going: "Despite the amount
of work we will all have to do, what personal priorities do
you want to make sure are not compromised? In other
words, what is most important for you from a personal
perspective as we embark on this work?" Team members
voluntarily disclosed challenges in their personal lives,
which they felt comfortable doing because of their prior
separate conversations with Terry. The meeting concluded with the team brainstorming about how business
and personal objectives could be reached at the same
time. Members decided, for instance, that they needed to
know how to do one another's jobs so that they could
cover if anyone had to miss work. They also decided that
they needed to constantly keep abreast of everyone's
schedules and personal demands so that no one would
be taken by surprise, and the flow of work would not be
disrupted, if a member was absent.

As the pilots progressed, weekly planning meetings
continued to focus on both business and personal priorities. Members did learn one another's jobs inside and
out, and constantly updated everyone on the demands of
their personal lives. As one team member said, "We
knew each other's home routines, school holidays, and
soccer practice schedules. It was easy to do this because

we talked about everything up front." The lengthy stretch needed for a christening in Paris or for a six-week vacation that had been booked a year in advance—and other personal time constraints—were known and accounted for as legitimate business issues.

As the pilots concluded, there could be no doubt that the team's results were impressive. All of their ambitious deadlines were met or beaten. Moreover, the fact that everyone knew everyone else's job added to the creativity and value of the team's output. Most important, the team achieved its goal of developing systems for knowledge transfer that could be used throughout the company worldwide. They were evaluated in a 360-degree process by their customers, team members, and their senior management sponsors. The project was successful from every business measure they had established.

Not surprisingly, the team members' lives and careers were enhanced by their experience on the task force. No one had to compromise personal priorities because of work. And, as one team member said, because of the openness and trust created within the team, "the project was the most satisfying work environment I have ever been in." Professionally, members of the team flourished after the project was completed. Terry, for instance, received a major promotion and now heads up the strategic-support function for one of the company's largest regions.

Getting Beyond the Status Quo

As we've said, the three principles are typically put into practice by managers "flying under the radar." Our next case, however, involves the manager of an HR department at a prominent accounting firm who actually used the principles to put the issues on the radar screen, thereby enhancing the performance of his organization's business-assurance department and the life of one of its senior associates, an aspiring novelist we'll call Jane.

Jane had joined the firm after graduating from college with a double major in accounting and English. She enjoyed her work—and was considered a strong performer by her superiors—but she also yearned to find time for her real passion, creative writing. After rummaging through the materials that were handed out back at her orientation, Jane came across a pamphlet that discussed the company's policy on alternative work schedules. She had hoped there would be a way to develop a schedule that would take advantage of the seasonal nature of the accounting business and allow her to carve out significant blocks of time for writing. But none of the examples of alternative schedules in the pamphlet came close to meeting her needs. Even though it felt risky to ask for something radically different, Jane approached Harry, the HR manager responsible for her department. In a way, there was no one else to turn to. Because of the project-based nature of Jane's work, the managers supervising her job were always changing. Much to her surprise, Harry was receptive and said he would be glad to work with Jane to craft a solution to her work-life dilemma.

Jane began by suggesting she reduce her workload from 12 to 8 clients. The change would mean that in the off-season she'd have sufficient chunks of time to focus on writing. Client by client, Harry and Jane decided which ones to keep and which to pass on to other associates. They then charted out the expected work for the upcoming year, making sure there would be enough time both for fulfilling her clients' needs and for writing.

At first, the plan seemed like a good one. Unfortunately, Jane quickly began to doubt how realistic it was. Often during her writing time, she would get a call from the central assignments department, putting her on another job. Although Jane knew she could legitimately decline those assignments because she had already completed the work she had contracted for, she was concerned that refusing work might have ramifications for her career later on. Hesitantly, she approached Harry a second time.

Harry was again receptive, inviting Gabriel, a member of the central assignments department, to join the discussions. The three of them then developed a method by which Jane's hours were logged so that there no longer would be any confusion about when she had extra time available for work and when the extra time was reserved for writing. Jane also suggested that she change the way she did her work. Could she try e-mailing and faxing her clients, she asked, instead of assuming that a face-to-face meeting was always necessary? Harry agreed to let her experiment.

The benefits of the new arrangement became apparent within the year, particularly with regard to Jane's capacity to contribute to the firm. With fewer clients, Jane felt more focused at work and thus more committed and effective. Previously, she had been moved from project to project and sometimes from crisis to crisis. Now she could plan her time in advance and concentrate on end results more creatively. In fact, she found that for the first time she had enough energy and time to reflect on better ways to get her projects done. Her clients responded positively; Jane's efficiency allowed her to work more quickly, which in some cases reduced their fees. And meanwhile, Jane was able to write two novels.

Three years later, still following this alternative work schedule, Jane was promoted to manager at the same time as others in her cohort. As a manager herself, Jane now practices the three principles. She believes they help her keep and motivate quality employees. Not only is it costly to replace a good employee, but, she notes, "people who are constantly under pressure will take the path of least resistance, doing things the way it was done last year instead of looking for ways to improve on the product." Furthermore, Jane points out that, unlike in other work groups at the company, "my group doesn't have to work weekends. Instead, we've found out everyone's parameters, discussed what work needs to get done, and focused on the end results."

Recently, Harry and Jane served together on a task force that's looking for ways to apply more broadly what they learned from practicing the three principles. They are exploring the development of a project database that would make it easier to anticipate the workload in advance and even out the assignments among the associates. They are looking into the possibility of defining expected work hours more explicitly. They believe that this will encourage a new attitude whereby excessive work hours will be seen not as a measure of commitment but as an indication of the need for better planning.

Although Jane and Harry are plainly aware of the benefits to the business of the approach they've developed, Jane is also absolutely clear about the personal benefits. "Neither activity, work nor writing, was appealing in isolation. I didn't want to be a starving writer, forced to write to earn a living. But I also felt that if I stopped practicing my writing, my creative side would die, and then the job would just become a job. Until we worked out this solution, I felt like it had to be an either-or choice, but now I see it doesn't have to be that way. Both sides can win."

A New Breed of Managers

If the three principles are so effective, why aren't they more widespread? There is no single answer. Some managers block the new approach to balancing work and life because they are bound by tradition and continue to value face time for its own sake. They believe that productivity is a function of time spent in the office—not energy invested in the work. Other managers are simply unaware that their employees might be able to bring skills and knowledge to their jobs from their lives beyond work. And still other managers consider the whole topic of striking a balance between work and personal life as a women's issue—in other words, not their problem.

We have also found that managers resist the three principles because they fear that taking an employee's personal priorities into account will create either a sense of entitlement or feelings of resentment. Take the case of Sarah and Hallie again. Once Hallie allowed Sarah to work at home to care for her ailing mother, these managers might reason, what's to stop everyone in the office from asking for some sort of special treatment to make his or her life more convenient or enjoyable? If we oblige, these managers might argue, we risk creating a slippery-slope situation in which the organization is expected to strike a work-life balance for every employee. If we don't, we are certain to anger people who feel slighted. Why should Sarah be allowed to work at home, another

employee may ask, if I still have to come into the office
when my child or husband is sick? What makes her more
deserving than me?

It's understandable that managers worry about setting off waves of entitlement and/or resentment. But
interestingly, the managers in our research who use the
three principles rarely run into that. Because these managers deal with all of their people individually, every one
of their employees does, in fact, receive "special" treatment in terms of a work plan that takes personal priorities into account. Therefore, there is less chance for
resentment to fester. As for entitlement, the enormous
loyalty these employees feel toward their managers usually outweighs it. Indeed, when a manager helps his or
her employees strike a work-life balance, they feel grateful more than anything else.

Even when managers are inclined to operate with the
three principles, many tell us that they don't because
they believe it would be impractical and complicated.
How time consuming it must be to delve into the varied
priorities and life roles of every employee, they argue.
And imagine how much energy it would take to create a
series of individual action plans that fulfill both professional and personal goals.

But we have found that, in reality, following the three
principles does not involve that much more time or
energy than managing in more traditional ways. Virtually all managers today are held accountable for developing their employees professionally—that is, they already
engage in discussions about what their people want and
need from work and what they are expected to contribute. To bring personal-life priorities and goals into
the conversation really only involves asking two or
three more questions. And often the answers to those

questions are so illuminating, they make the development process more honest—and more efficient.

Sometimes the "work" of the three principles can be delegated to the employees themselves, who can apply them personally and to their dealings with one another. In fact, we have seen that people become quickly engaged in this process as they come to realize that the solutions they develop will benefit both the business and their own lives. Consequently, the principles need not sap any more time or energy than conducting management as usual.

Out from Under the Radar

No two companies—indeed, no two managers— approach the relationship between work and personal life exactly the same way. But it is fair to say that all organizational practices fall along a continuum. On one end is the *trade-off* approach, whereby either the business wins or personal life wins, but not both. Further along is the *integrated* approach, in which employee and manager work together to find ways to meet both the company's and the employee's needs. That approach is indeed becoming more common, as an increasing number of companies use "life friendly" policies to attract and retain talented people.

Taken together, the three principles fall at the far end of the continuum—the *leveraged* approach, in which the practices used to strike a work-life balance actually add value to the business. Not only do the three principles seem to help people live more satisfying personal lives, but they also help identify inefficiencies in work processes and illuminate better ways to get work done. Think of the pharmaceutical company's command center, for example. Using the three principles, its staff created a new and successful solution to its managerial problems that neither the trade-off nor the integrated approach could have achieved.

The growing cadre of managers who use the three principles to help their employees strike a work-life balance typically do so without official sanction. But perhaps as the business impact of their approach becomes better known and understood, a shift will occur. Managers who once flew below the radar will themselves become beacons of change.

Where to Begin

PUTTING THE THREE PRINCIPLES into practice does not happen overnight. It can't—the changes required by this new approach are too substantial to be instituted without stops and starts and periods of evaluation. Therefore, when managers ask us how to get started, we often suggest that they begin by applying the principles to one employee. Think of Steve, the senior executive who once expected his staff to work from 7 A.M. to 10 P.M. He used the three principles to help one person—Jim—strike a meaningful balance between work and personal life. The arrangement—and its successful impact on both Jim and the business—gave Steve the experience and the confidence he needed to apply the three principles more broadly. Eventually, the principles became the foundation of his management style.

A second way to get started with the principles is to initiate an organizational dialogue about integrating work and personal life goals. In small-team settings, a manager might even lead the process of creating a work-life philosophy statement. We have seen such dialogues facilitate the implementation of the principles by bringing to light thorny issues such as the organization's level of commitment to striking a work-life balance or employees' fears about sharing private information about their personal priorities and life roles.

As a third starting point, we suggest that managers try applying the three principles to themselves to find out how well they personally have leveraged work and personal life. First, a manager might ask, "How well do I clarify my own life goals? Do I know where work falls in my list of priorities? What trade-offs am I willing to make to achieve my goals?"

Second, a manager might consider, "Do I understand my varied life roles—such as parent, child, cub scout master—in terms of how they overlap and when they must be kept separate? That is, have I considered what skills and knowledge can be transferred from one role to another, and have I explicitly formulated the boundaries of each role?" Some executives, for instance, will not check voice mail on weekends; others let their work and personal lives blend.

And finally, a manager can explore his or her comfort level with the third principle of continual experimentation by asking, "Do I regularly challenge the way I myself approach tasks, both at work and at home? How do I react when other people suggest new ways to get things done? Am I defensive or intrigued?"

A self-assessment is useful because it shows managers who want to embark on the journey of striking a balance between work and personal life how sensitive they may or may not be to the struggles of employees trying to do the same. Does that mean people who don't have their own house in order should avoid managing with the principles? Not necessarily, but they should be aware that striking a work-life balance, like many other aspects of effective management, can take time, energy, and commitment. Given its added value, however, the process appears to be well worth the investment.

Originally published in November–December 1998
Reprint 98605

Making Differences Matter

A New Paradigm for Managing Diversity

DAVID A. THOMAS AND ROBIN J. ELY

Executive Summary

DIVERSITY EFFORTS IN the workplace have been under-
taken with great goodwill, but, ironically, they often end
up fueling tensions. They rarely spur the leaps in organizational effectiveness that are possible. Two paradigms
for diversity are responsible, but a new one is showing it
can address the problem.

The discrimination-and-fairness paradigm is based on
the recognition that discrimination is wrong. Under it,
progress is measured by how well the company
achieves its recruitment and retention goals. The paradigm idealizes assimilation and color- and gender-blind
conformism. The access-and-legitimacy paradigm, on the
other hand, celebrates differences. Under it, organizations seek access to a more diverse clientele, matching
their demographics to targeted consumers. But that

paradigm can leave employees of different identity-group affiliations feeling marginalized or exploited.

In companies with the right kind of leadership, a third paradigm is showing that beneficial learning takes place and organizations become more effective in fulfilling their missions if employees are encouraged to tap their differences for creative ideas. If all or most of eight preconditions are in place, the opportunities for growth are almost unlimited.

Leaders in third-paradigm companies are proactive about learning from diversity; they encourage people to make explicit use of cultural experience at work; they fight all forms of dominance and subordination, including those generated by one functional group acting superior to another; and they ensure that the inevitable tensions that come from a genuine effort to make way for diversity are acknowledged and resolved with sensitivity.

W HY SHOULD COMPANIES concern themselves with diversity? Until recently, many managers answered this question with the assertion that discrimination is wrong, both legally and morally. But today managers are voicing a second notion as well. A more diverse work-force, they say, will increase organizational effectiveness. It will lift morale, bring greater access to new segments of the marketplace, and enhance productivity. In short, they claim, diversity will be good for business.

Yet if this is true—and we believe it is—where are the positive impacts of diversity? Numerous and varied initiatives to increase diversity in corporate America have been under way for more than two decades. Rarely, however, have those efforts spurred leaps in organizational effectiveness. Instead, many attempts to increase diversity in the workplace have backfired, sometimes even heightening tensions among employees and hindering a company's performance.

This article offers an explanation for why diversity efforts are not fulfilling their promise and presents a new paradigm for understanding—and leveraging—diversity. It is our belief that there is a distinct way to unleash the powerful benefits of a diverse workforce. Although these benefits include increased profitability, they go beyond financial measures to encompass learning, creativity, flexibility, organizational and individual growth, and the ability of a company to adjust rapidly and successfully to market changes. The desired transformation, however, requires a fundamental change in the attitudes and behaviors of an organization's leadership. And that will come only when senior managers abandon an underlying and flawed assumption about diversity and replace it with a broader understanding.

Most people assume that workplace diversity is about increasing racial, national, gender, or class representation—in other words, recruiting and retaining more people from traditionally underrepresented "identity groups." Taking this commonly held assumption as a starting point, we set out six years ago to investigate its link to organizational effectiveness. We soon found that thinking of diversity simply in terms of identity-group representation inhibited effectiveness.

Organizations usually take one of two paths in managing diversity. In the name of equality and fairness, they encourage (and expect) women and people of color to blend in. Or they set them apart in jobs that relate specifically to their backgrounds, assigning them, for example, to areas that require them to interface with clients or customers of the same identity group. African American M.B.A.'s often find themselves marketing products to inner-city communities; Hispanics frequently market to Hispanics or work for Latin American subsidiaries. In those kinds of cases, companies are operating on the assumption that the main virtue identity groups have to offer is a knowledge of their own people. This assumption is limited—and limiting—and detrimental to diversity efforts.

What we suggest here is that diversity goes beyond increasing the number of different identity-group affiliations on the payroll to recognizing that such an effort is merely the first step in managing a diverse workforce for the organization's utmost benefit. Diversity should be understood as *the varied perspectives and approaches to work* that members of different identity groups bring.

Women, Hispanics, Asian Americans, African Americans, Native Americans—these groups and others outside the mainstream of corporate America don't bring with them just their "insider information." They bring different, important, and competitively relevant knowledge and perspectives about how to actually *do work*— how to design processes, reach goals, frame tasks, create effective teams, communicate ideas, and lead. When allowed to, members of these groups can help companies grow and improve by challenging basic assumptions about an organization's functions, strategies, operations, practices, and procedures. And in doing so, they are able to bring more of their whole selves to the workplace and identify more fully with the work they do, setting in motion a virtuous circle. Certainly, individuals can be expected to contribute to a company their firsthand familiarity with niche markets. But only when companies start thinking about diversity more holistically—as providing fresh and meaningful approaches to work—and stop assuming that diversity relates simply to how a person looks or where he or she comes from, will they be able to reap its full rewards.

Two perspectives have guided most diversity initiatives to date: the *discrimination-and-fairness paradigm* and the *access-and-legitimacy paradigm*. But we have identified a new, emerging approach to this complex management issue. This approach, which we call the *learning-and-effectiveness paradigm,* incorporates aspects of the first two paradigms but goes beyond them by concretely connecting diversity to approaches to work. Our goal is to help business leaders see what their own approach to diversity currently is and how it may already have influenced their companies' diversity efforts. Managers can learn to assess whether they need to change their diversity initiatives and, if so, how to accomplish that change.

The following discussion will also cite several examples of how connecting the new definition of diversity to the actual *doing* of work has led some organizations to markedly better performance. The organizations differ in many ways—none are in the same industry, for instance—but they are united by one similarity: Their leaders realize that increasing demographic variation does not in itself increase organizational effectiveness. They realize that it is *how* a company defines diversity—and *what it does* with the experiences of being a diverse organization—that delivers on the promise.

The Discrimination-and-Fairness Paradigm

Using the discrimination-and-fairness paradigm is perhaps thus far the dominant way of understanding diversity. Leaders who look at diversity through this lens usually focus on equal opportunity, fair treatment, recruitment, and compliance with federal Equal Employment Opportunity requirements. The paradigm's underlying logic can be expressed as follows:

> *Prejudice has kept members of certain demographic groups out of organizations such as ours. As a matter of fairness and to comply with federal mandates, we need to work toward restructuring the makeup of our organization to let it more closely reflect that of society. We need managerial processes that ensure that all our employees are treated equally and with respect and that some are not given unfair advantage over others.*

Although it resembles the thinking behind traditional affirmative-action efforts, the discrimination-and-fairness paradigm does go beyond a simple concern with numbers. Companies that operate with this philosophical orientation often institute mentoring and career-development programs specifically for the women and people of color in their ranks and train other employees to respect cultural differences. Under this paradigm, nevertheless, progress in diversity is measured by how well the company achieves its recruitment and retention goals rather than by the degree to which conditions in the company allow employees to draw on their personal assets and perspectives to do their work more effectively. The staff, one might say, gets diversified, but the work does not.

What are some of the common characteristics of companies that have used the discrimination-and-fairness paradigm successfully to increase their demographic diversity? Our research indicates that they are usually run by leaders who value due process and equal treatment of all employees and who have the authority to use top-down directives to enforce initiatives based

on those attitudes. Such companies are often bureaucratic in structure, with control processes in place for
monitoring, measuring, and rewarding individual performance. And finally, they are often organizations with
entrenched, easily observable cultures, in which values
like fairness are widespread and deeply inculcated and
codes of conduct are clear and unambiguous. (Perhaps
the most extreme example of an organization in which
all these factors are at work is the United States Army.)

Without doubt, there are benefits to this paradigm: it
does tend to increase demographic diversity in an organization, and it often succeeds in promoting fair treatment. But it also has significant limitations. The first of
these is that its color-blind, gender-blind ideal is to some
degree built on the implicit assumption that "we are all
the same" or "we aspire to being all the same." Under this
paradigm, it is not desirable for diversification of the
workforce to influence the organization's work or culture. The company should operate as if every person
were of the same race, gender, and nationality. It is
unlikely that leaders who manage diversity under this
paradigm will explore how people's differences generate
a potential diversity of effective ways of working, leading,
viewing the market, managing people, and learning.

Not only does the discrimination-and-fairness
paradigm insist that everyone is the same, but, with its
emphasis on equal treatment, it puts pressure on
employees to make sure that important differences
among them do not count. Genuine disagreements about
work definition, therefore, are sometimes wrongly interpreted through this paradigm's fairness-unfairness
lens—especially when honest disagreements are accom-
panied by tense debate. A female employee who insists,
for example, that a company's advertising strategy is not

appropriate for all ethnic segments in the marketplace might feel she is violating the code of assimilation upon which the paradigm is built. Moreover, if she were then to defend her opinion by citing, let us say, her personal knowledge of the ethnic group the company wanted to reach, she might risk being perceived as importing inappropriate attitudes into an organization that prides itself on being blind to cultural differences.

Workplace paradigms channel organizational thinking in powerful ways. By limiting the ability of employees to acknowledge openly their work-related but culturally based differences, the paradigm actually undermines the organization's capacity to learn about and improve its own strategies, processes, and practices. And it also keeps people from identifying strongly and personally with their work—a critical source of motivation and self-regulation in any business environment.

As an illustration of the paradigm's weaknesses, consider the case of Iversen Dunham, an international consulting firm that focuses on foreign and domestic economic-development policy. (Like all the examples in this article, the company is real, but its name is disguised.) Not long ago, the firm's managers asked us to help them understand why race relations had become a divisive issue precisely at a time when Iversen was receiving accolades for its diversity efforts. Indeed, other organizations had even begun to use the firm to benchmark their own diversity programs.

Iversen's diversity efforts had begun in the early 1970s, when senior managers decided to pursue greater racial and gender diversity in the firm's higher ranks. (The firm's leaders were strongly committed to the cause of social justice.) Women and people of color were hired and charted on career paths toward becoming project leaders. High performers among those who had left the firm were persuaded to return in senior roles. By 1989, about 50% of Iversen's project leaders and professionals were women, and 30% were people of color. The 13-member management committee, once exclusively white and male, included five women and four people of color. Additionally, Iversen had developed a strong contingent of foreign nationals.

It was at about this time, however, that tensions began to surface. Senior managers found it hard to believe that, after all the effort to create a fair and mutually respectful work community, some staff members could still be claiming that Iversen had racial discrimination problems. The management invited us to study the firm and deliver an outsider's assessment of its problem.

We had been inside the firm for only a short time when it became clear that Iversen's leaders viewed the dynamics of diversity through the lens of the discrimination-and-fairness paradigm. But where they saw racial discord, we discerned clashing approaches to the actual work of consulting. Why? Our research showed that tensions were strongest among midlevel project leaders. Surveys and interviews indicated that white project leaders welcomed demographic diversity as a general sign of progress but that they also thought the new employees were somehow changing the company, pulling it away from its original culture and its mission. Common criticisms were that African American and Hispanic staff made problems too complex by linking issues the organization had traditionally regarded as unrelated and that they brought on projects that seemed to require greater cultural sensitivity. White male project leaders also complained that their peers who were women and people of color were undermining one of Iversen's traditional

strengths: its hard-core quantitative orientation. For
instance, minority project leaders had suggested that
Iversen consultants collect information and seek input
from others in the client company besides senior managers—that is, from the rank and file and from middle
managers. Some had urged Iversen to expand its consulting approach to include the gathering and analysis of
qualitative data through interviewing and observation.
Indeed, these project leaders had even challenged one of
Iversen's long-standing, core assumptions: that the firm's
reports were objective. They urged Iversen Dunham to
recognize and address the subjective aspect of its analy-
ses; the firm could, for example, include in its reports to
clients dissenting Iversen views, if any existed.

For their part, project leaders who were women and
people of color felt that they were not accorded the same
level of authority to carry out that work as their white
male peers. Moreover, they sensed that those peers were
skeptical of their opinions, and they resented that doubts
were not voiced openly.

Meanwhile, there also was some concern expressed
about tension between white managers and nonwhite
subordinates, who claimed they were being treated
unfairly. But our analysis suggested that the manager-
subordinate conflicts were not numerous enough to
warrant the attention they were drawing from top management. We believed it was significant that senior
managers found it easier to focus on this second type of
conflict than on mid level conflicts about project choice
and project definition. Indeed, Iversen Dunham's focus
seemed to be a result of the firm's reliance on its particular diversity paradigm and the emphasis on fairness and
equality. It was relatively easy to diagnose problems in

light of those concepts and to devise a solution: just get managers to treat their subordinates more fairly.

In contrast, it was difficult to diagnose peer-to-peer tensions in the framework of this model. Such conflicts were about the very nature of Iversen's work, not simply unfair treatment. Yes, they were related to identity-group affiliations, but they were not symptomatic of classic racism. It was Iversen's paradigm that led managers to interpret them as such. Remember, we were asked to assess what was supposed to be a racial discrimination problem. Iversen's discrimination-and-fairness paradigm had created a kind of cognitive blind spot; and, as a result, the company's leadership could not frame the problem accurately or solve it effectively. Instead, the company needed a cultural shift—it needed to grasp what to do with its diversity once it had achieved the numbers. If all Iversen Dunham employees were to contribute to the fullest extent, the company would need a paradigm that would encourage open and explicit discussion of what identity-group differences really mean and how they can be used as sources of individual and organizational effectiveness.

Today, mainly because of senior managers' resistance to such a cultural transformation, Iversen continues to struggle with the tensions arising from the diversity of its workforce.

The Access-and-Legitimacy Paradigm

In the competitive climate of the 1980s and 1990s, a new rhetoric and rationale for managing diversity emerged. If the discrimination-and-fairness paradigm can be said to have idealized assimilation and color- and gender-blind conformism, the access-and-legitimacy paradigm was predicated on the acceptance and celebration of differences. The underlying motivation of the access-and-legitimacy paradigm can be expressed this way:

> *We are living in an increasingly multicultural country, and new ethnic groups are quickly gaining consumer power. Our company needs a demographically more diverse workforce to help us gain access to these differentiated segments. We need employees with multilingual skills in order to understand and serve our customers better and to gain legitimacy with them. Diversity isn't just fair; it makes business sense.*

Where this paradigm has taken hold, organizations have pushed for access to—and legitimacy with—a more diverse clientele by matching the demographics of the organization to those of critical consumer or constituent groups. In some cases, the effort has led to substantial increases in organizational diversity. In investment banks, for example, municipal finance departments have long led corporate finance departments in pursuing demographic diversity because of the typical makeup of the administration of city halls and county boards. Many consumer-products companies that have used market segmentation based on gender, racial, and other demographic differences have also frequently created dedicated marketing positions for each segment. The paradigm has therefore led to new professional and managerial opportunities for women and people of color.

What are the common characteristics of organizations that have successfully used the access-and-legitimacy paradigm to increase their demographic diversity? There is but one: such companies almost always operate in a business environment in which there is increased diversity among customers, clients, or the labor pool—and therefore a clear opportunity or an imminent threat to the company.

Again, the paradigm has its strengths. Its market-based motivation and the potential for competitive advantage that it suggests are often qualities an entire company can understand and therefore support. But the paradigm is perhaps more notable for its limitations. In their pursuit of niche markets, access-and-legitimacy organizations tend to emphasize the role of cultural differences in a company without really analyzing those differences to see how they actually affect the work that is done. Whereas discrimination-and fairness leaders are too quick to subvert differences in the interest of preserving harmony, access-and-legitimacy leaders are too quick to push staff with niche capabilities into differentiated pigeonholes without trying to understand what those capabilities really are and how they could be integrated into the company's mainstream work. To illustrate our point, we present the case of Access Capital.

Access Capital International is a U.S. investment bank that in the early 1980s launched an aggressive plan to expand into Europe. Initially, however, Access encountered serious problems opening offices in international markets; the people from the United States who were installed abroad lacked credibility, were ignorant of local cultural norms and market conditions, and simply couldn't seem to connect with native clients. Access responded by hiring Europeans who had attended North American business schools and by assigning them in teams to the foreign offices. This strategy was a marked success. Before long, the leaders of Access could take enormous pride in the fact that their European operations were highly profitable and staffed by a truly international corps of professionals. They took to calling the company "the best investment bank in the world."

Several years passed. Access's foreign offices continued to thrive, but some leaders were beginning to sense that the company was not fully benefiting from its diversity efforts. Indeed, some even suspected that the bank had made itself vulnerable because of how it had chosen to manage diversity. A senior executive from the United States explains:

> *If the French team all resigned tomorrow, what would we do? I'm not sure what we could do! We've never attempted to learn what these differences and cultural competencies really are, how they change the process of doing business. What is the German country team actually doing? We don't know. We know they're good, but we don't know the subtleties of how they do what they do. We assumed— and I think correctly—that culture makes a difference, but that's about as far as we went. We hired Europeans with American M.B.A.'s because we didn't know why we couldn't do business in Europe—we just assumed there was something cultural about why we couldn't connect. And ten years later, we still don't know what it is. If we knew, then perhaps we could take it and teach it. Which part of the investment banking process is universal and which part of it draws upon particular cultural competencies? What are the commonalities and differences? I may not be German, but maybe I could do better at understanding what it means to be an American doing business in Germany. Our company's biggest failing is that the department heads in London and the directors of the various country teams have never talked about these cultural identity issues openly. We knew enough to use people's cultural strengths, as it were, but we never seemed to learn from them.*

Access's story makes an important point about the main limitation of the access-and-legitimacy paradigm: under its influence, the motivation for diversity usually emerges from very immediate and often crisis-oriented needs for access and legitimacy—in this case, the need to broker deals in European markets. However, once the organization appears to be achieving its goal, the leaders seldom go on to identify and analyze the culturally based skills, beliefs, and practices that worked so well. Nor do they consider how the organization can incorporate and learn from those skills, beliefs, or practices in order to capitalize on diversity in the long run.

Under the access and legitimacy paradigm, it was as if the bank's country teams had become little spin-off companies in their own right, doing their own exotic, slightly mysterious cultural-diversity thing in a niche market of their own, using competencies that for some reason could not become more fully integrated into the larger organization's understanding of itself. Difference was valued within Access Capital—hence the development of country teams in the first place—but not valued enough that the organization would try to integrate it into the very core of its culture and into its business practices.

Finally, the access-and-legitimacy paradigm can leave some employees feeling exploited. Many organizations using this paradigm have diversified only in those areas in which they interact with particular niche-market segments. In time, many individuals recruited for this function have come to feel devalued and used as they begin to sense that opportunities in other parts of the organization are closed to them. Often the larger organization regards the experience of these employees as more limited or specialized, even though many of them in fact started their careers in the mainstream market before moving to special markets where their cultural backgrounds were a recognized asset. Also, many of these people say that when companies have needed to downsize or narrow their marketing focus, it is the special departments that are often the first to go. That situation creates tenuous and ultimately untenable career paths for employees in the special departments.

The Emerging Paradigm: Connecting Diversity to Work Perspectives

Recently, in the course of our research, we have encountered a small number of organizations that, having relied initially on one of the above paradigms to guide their diversity efforts, have come to believe that they are not making the most of their own pluralism. These organizations, like Access Capital, recognize that employees frequently make decisions and choices at work that draw upon their cultural background—choices made because of their identity-group affiliations. The companies have also developed an outlook on diversity that enables them to *incorporate* employees' perspectives into the main work of the organization and to enhance work by rethinking primary tasks and redefining markets, products, strategies, missions, business practices, and even cultures. Such companies are using the learning-and-effectiveness paradigm for managing diversity and, by doing so, are tapping diversity's true benefits.

A case in point is Dewey & Levin, a small public-interest law firm located in a northeastern U.S. city. Although Dewey & Levin had long been a profitable practice, by the mid-1980s its all-white legal staff had become concerned that the women they represented in employment-related disputes were exclusively white. The firm's attorneys viewed that fact as a deficiency in light of their mandate to advocate on behalf of all women. Using the thinking behind the access-and-legitimacy paradigm, they also saw it as bad for business.

Shortly thereafter, the firm hired a Hispanic female attorney. The partners' hope, simply put, was that she would bring in clients from her own community and also demonstrate the firm's commitment to representing all women. But something even bigger than that happened. The new attorney introduced ideas to Dewey & Levin about what kinds of cases it should take on. Senior managers were open to those ideas and pursued them with great success. More women of color were hired, and they, too, brought fresh perspectives. The firm now pursues cases that its previously all white legal staff would not have thought relevant or appropriate because the link between the firm's mission and the employment issues involved in the cases would not have been obvious to them. For example, the firm has pursued precedent-setting litigation that challenges English-only policies— an area that it once would have ignored because such policies did not fall under the purview of traditional affirmative-action work. Yet it now sees a link between English-only policies and employment issues for a large group of women—primarily recent immigrants—whom it had previously failed to serve adequately. As one of the white principals explains, the demographic composition of Dewey & Levin "has affected the work in terms of expanding notions of what are [relevant] issues and taking on issues and framing them in creative ways that would have never been done [with an all-white staff]. It's really changed the substance—and in that sense enhanced the quality—of our work."

Dewey & Levin's increased business success has reinforced its commitment to diversity. In addition, people of color at the firm uniformly report feeling respected, not simply "brought along as window dressing." Many of the new attorneys say their perspectives are heard with a kind of openness and interest they have never experienced before in a work setting. Not surprisingly, the firm has had little difficulty attracting and retaining a competent and diverse professional staff.

If the discrimination-and-fairness paradigm is organized around the theme of assimilation—in which the aim is to achieve a demographically representative workforce whose members treat one another exactly the same—then the access-and-legitimacy paradigm can be regarded as coalescing around an almost opposite concept: differentiation, in which the objective is to place different people where their demographic characteristics match those of important constituents and markets.

The emerging paradigm, in contrast to both, organizes itself around the overarching theme of integration. Assimilation goes too far in pursuing sameness. Differentiation, as we have shown, overshoots in the other direction. The new model for managing diversity transcends both. Like the fairness paradigm, it promotes equal opportunity for all individuals. And like the access paradigm, it acknowledges cultural differences among people and recognizes the value in those differences. Yet this new model for managing diversity lets the organization internalize differences among employees so that it learns and grows because of them. Indeed, with the model fully in place, members of the organization can say, We are all on the same team, with our differences—not *despite* them.

Eight Preconditions for Making the Paradigm Shift

Dewey & Levin may be atypical in its eagerness to open itself up to change and engage in a long-term transformation process. We remain convinced, however, that unless organizations that are currently in the grip of the other two paradigms can revise their view of diversity so as to avoid cognitive blind spots, opportunities will be missed, tensions will most likely be misdiagnosed, and companies will continue to find the potential benefits of diversity elusive.

Hence the question arises: What is it about the law firm of Dewey & Levin and other emerging third-paradigm companies that enables them to make the most of their diversity? Our research suggests that there are eight preconditions that help to position organizations to use identity group differences in the service of organizational learning, growth, and renewal.

1. **The leadership must understand that a diverse workforce will embody different perspectives and approaches to work, and must truly value variety of opinion and insight.** We know of a financial services company that once assumed that the only successful sales model was one that utilized aggressive, rapid-fire cold calls. (Indeed, its incentive system rewarded salespeople in large part for the number of calls made.) An internal review of the company's diversity initiatives, however, showed that the company's first- and third-most-profitable employees were women who were most likely to use a sales technique based on the slow but sure building of relationships. The company's top management has now made the link between different identity groups and different approaches to how work gets done and has come to see that there is more than one right way to get positive results.

2. **The leadership must recognize both the learning opportunities and the challenges that the**

expression of different perspectives presents for an organization. In other words, the second precondition is a leadership that is committed to persevering during the long process of learning and relearning that the new paradigm requires.

3. **The organizational culture must create an expectation of high standards of performance from everyone.** Such a culture isn't one that expects less from some employees than from others. Some organizations expect women and people of color to underperform—a negative assumption that too often becomes a self-fulfilling prophecy. To move to the third paradigm, a company must believe that all its members can and should contribute fully.

4. **The organizational culture must stimulate personal development.** Such a culture brings out people's full range of useful knowledge and skills—usually through the careful design of jobs that allow people to grow and develop but also through training and education programs.

5. **The organizational culture must encourage openness.** Such a culture instills a high tolerance for debate and supports constructive conflict on work-related matters.

6. **The culture must make workers feel valued.** If this precondition is met, workers feel committed to—and empowered within—the organization and therefore feel comfortable taking the initiative to apply their skills and experiences in new ways to enhance their job performance.

7. **The organization must have a well-articulated and widely understood mission.** Such a mission enables people to be clear about what the company is trying to accomplish. It grounds and guides discussions about work-related changes that staff members might suggest. Being clear about the company's mission helps keep discussions about work differences from degenerating into debates about the validity of people's perspectives. A clear mission provides a focal point that keeps the discussion centered on accomplishment of goals.

8. **The organization must have a relatively egalitarian, nonbureaucratic structure.** It's important to have a structure that promotes the exchange of ideas and welcomes constructive challenges to the usual way of doing things—from any employee with valuable experience. Forward-thinking leaders in bureaucratic organizations must retain the organization's efficiency-promoting control systems and chains of command while finding ways to reshape the change-resisting mind-set of the classic bureaucratic model. They need to separate the enabling elements of bureaucracy (the ability to get things done) from the disabling elements of bureaucracy (those that create resistance to experimentation).

First Interstate Bank: A Paradigm Shift in Progress

All eight preconditions do not have to be in place in order to begin a shift from the first or second diversity orientations toward the learning-and-effectiveness paradigm.

But most should be. First Interstate Bank, a midsize bank operating in a midwestern city, illustrates this point.

First Interstate, admittedly, is not a typical bank. Its client base is a minority community, and its mission is expressly to serve that base through "the development of a highly talented workforce." The bank is unique in other ways: its leadership welcomes constructive criticism; its structure is relatively egalitarian and nonbureaucratic; and its culture is open-minded. Nevertheless, First Interstate had long enforced a policy that loan officers had to hold college degrees. Those without were hired only for support-staff jobs and were never promoted beyond or outside support functions.

Two years ago, however, the support staff began to challenge the policy. Many of them had been with First Interstate for many years and, with the company's active support, had improved their skills through training. Others had expanded their skills on the job, again with the bank's encouragement, learning to run credit checks, prepare presentations for clients, and even calculate the algorithms necessary for many loan decisions. As a result, some people on the support staff were doing many of the same tasks as loan officers. Why, then, they wondered, couldn't they receive commensurate rewards in title and compensation?

This questioning led to a series of contentious meetings between the support staff and the bank's senior managers. It soon became clear that the problem called for managing diversity—diversity based not on race or gender but on class. The support personnel were uniformly from lower socioeconomic communities than were the college-educated loan officers. Regardless, the principle was the same as for race- or gender-based diversity problems. The support staff had different ideas about how the work of the bank should be done. They argued that those among them with the requisite skills should be allowed to rise through the ranks to professional positions, and they believed their ideas were not being heard or accepted.

Their beliefs challenged assumptions that the company's leadership had long held about which employees should have the authority to deal with customers and about how much responsibility administrative employees should ultimately receive. In order to take up this challenge, the bank would have to be open to exploring the requirements that a new perspective would impose on it. It would need to consider the possibility of mapping out an educational and career path for people without degrees—a path that could put such workers on the road to becoming loan officers. In other words, the leadership would have to transform itself willingly and embrace fluidity in policies that in times past had been clearly stated and unquestioningly held.

Today the bank's leadership is undergoing just such a transformation. The going, however, is far from easy. The bank's senior managers now must look beyond the tensions and acrimony sparked by the debate over differing work perspectives and consider the bank's new direction an important learning and growth opportunity.

Shift Complete: Third-Paradigm Companies in Action

First Interstate is a shift in progress; but, in addition to Dewey & Levin, there are several organizations we know of for which the shift is complete. In these cases, company leaders have played a critical role as facilitators and tone setters. We have observed in particular that in organizations that have adopted the new perspective, leaders and managers—and, following in their tracks, employees in general—are taking four kinds of action.

THEY ARE MAKING THE MENTAL CONNECTION

First, in organizations that have adopted the new perspective, the leaders are actively seeking opportunities to explore how identity-group differences affect relationships among workers and affect the way work gets done. They are investing considerable time and energy in understanding how identity-group memberships take on social meanings in the organization and how those meanings manifest themselves in the way work is defined, assigned, and accomplished. When there is no proactive search to understand, then learning from diversity, if it happens at all, can occur only reactively— that is, in response to diversity-related crises.

The situation at Iversen Dunham illustrates the missed opportunities resulting from that scenario. Rather than seeing differences in the way project leaders defined and approached their work as an opportunity to gain new insights and develop new approaches to achieving its mission, the firm remained entrenched in its traditional ways, able to arbitrate such differences only by thinking about what was fair and what was racist. With this quite limited view of the role race can play in an organization, discussions about the topic become fraught with fear and defensiveness, and everyone misses out on insights about how race might influence work in positive ways.

A second case, however, illustrates how some leaders using the new paradigm have been able to envision—and make—the connection between cultural diversity and the company's work. A vice president of Mastiff, a large national insurance company, received a complaint from one of the managers in her unit, an African American man. The manager wanted to demote an African American woman he had hired for a leadership position from another Mastiff division just three months before. He told the vice president he was profoundly disappointed with the performance of his new hire.

"I hired her because I was pretty certain she had tremendous leadership skill," he said. "I knew she had a management style that was very open and empowering. I was also sure she'd have a great impact on the rest of the management team. But she hasn't done any of that."

Surprised, the vice president tried to find out from him what he thought the problem was, but she was not getting any answers that she felt really defined or illuminated the root of the problem. Privately, it puzzled her that someone would decide to demote a 15-year veteran of the company—and a minority woman at that—so soon after bringing her to his unit.

The vice president probed further. In the course of the conversation, the manager happened to mention that he knew the new employee from church and was familiar with the way she handled leadership there and in other community settings. In those less formal situations, he had seen her perform as an extremely effective, sensitive, and influential leader.

That is when the vice president made an interpretive leap. "If that's what you know about her," the vice president said to the manager, "then the question for us is, why can't she bring those skills to work here?" The vice president decided to arrange a meeting with all three present to ask this very question directly. In the meeting, the African American woman explained, "I didn't think I would last long if I acted that way here. My personal style of leadership—that particular style—works well if you have the permission to do it fully; then you can just do it and not have to look over your shoulder."

Pointing to the manager who had planned to fire her, she added, "He's right. The style of leadership I use outside this company can definitely be effective. But I've been at Mastiff for 15 years. I know this organization, and I know if I brought that piece of myself—if I became that authentic—I just wouldn't survive here."

What this example illustrates is that the vice president's learning-and-effectiveness paradigm led her to explore and then make the link between cultural diversity and work style. What was occurring, she realized, was a mismatch between the cultural background of the recently promoted woman and the cultural environment of her work setting. It had little to do with private attitudes or feelings, or gender issues, or some inherent lack of leadership ability. The source of the underperformance was that the newly promoted woman had a certain style and the organization's culture did not support her in expressing it comfortably. The vice president's paradigm led her to ask new questions and to seek out new information, but, more important, it also led her to interpret existing information differently.

The two senior managers began to realize that part of the African American woman's inability to see herself as a leader at work was that she had for so long been undervalued in the organization. And, in a sense, she had become used to splitting herself off from who she was in her own community. In the 15 years she had been at Mastiff, she had done her job well as an individual contributor, but she had never received any signals that her bosses wanted her to draw on her cultural competencies in order to lead effectively.

THEY ARE LEGITIMATING OPEN DISCUSSION

Leaders and managers who have adopted the new paradigm are taking the initiative to "green light" open discussion about how identity-group memberships inform and influence an employee's experience and the organization's behavior. They are encouraging people to make *explicit* use of background cultural experience and the pools of knowledge gained outside the organization to inform and enhance their work. Individuals often do use their cultural competencies at work, but in a closeted, almost embarrassed, way. The unfortunate result is that the opportunity for collective and organizational learning and improvement is lost.

The case of a Chinese woman who worked as a chemist at Torinno Food Company illustrates this point. Linda was part of a product development group at Torinno when a problem arose with the flavoring of a new soup. After the group had made a number of scientific attempts to correct the problem, Linda came up with the solution by "setting aside my chemistry and drawing on my understanding of Chinese cooking." She did not, however, share with her colleagues—all of them white males—the real source of her inspiration for the solution for fear that it would set her apart or that they might consider her unprofessional. Overlaid on the cultural issue, of course, was a gender issue (women cooking) as well as a work-family issue (women doing *home* cooking in a chemistry lab). All of these themes had erected unspoken boundaries that Linda knew could be career-damaging for her to cross. After solving the problem, she simply went back to the so-called scientific way of doing things.

Senior managers at Torinno Foods in fact had made a substantial commitment to diversifying the workforce through a program designed to teach employees to value the contributions of all its members. Yet Linda's perceptions indicate that, in the actual day-to-day context of work, the program had failed—and in precisely one of those areas where it would have been important for it to have worked. It had failed to affirm someone's identity-group experiences as a legitimate source of insight into her work. It is likely that this organization will miss future opportunities to take full advantage of the talent of employees such as Linda. When people believe that they must suggest and apply their ideas covertly, the organization also misses opportunities to discuss, debate, refine, and build on those ideas fully. In addition, because individuals like Linda will continue to think that they must hide parts of themselves in order to fit in, they will find it difficult to engage fully not only in their work but also in their workplace relationships. That kind of situation can breed resentment and misunderstanding, fueling tensions that can further obstruct productive work relationships.

THEY ACTIVELY WORK AGAINST FORMS OF DOMINANCE AND SUBORDINATION THAT INHIBIT FULL CONTRIBUTION

Companies in which the third paradigm is emerging have leaders and managers who take responsibility for removing the barriers that block employees from using the full range of their competencies, cultural or otherwise. Racism, homophobia, sexism, and sexual harassment are the most obvious forms of dominance that decrease individual and organizational effectiveness—and third-paradigm leaders have zero tolerance for them. In addition, the leaders are aware that organizations can create their own unique patterns of dominance and subordination based on the presumed superiority and entitlement of some groups over others. It is not uncommon, for instance, to find organizations in which one functional area considers itself better than another. Members of the presumed inferior group frequently describe the organization in the very terms used by those who experience identity-group discrimination. Regardless of the source of the oppression, the result is diminished performance and commitment from employees.

What can leaders do to prevent those kinds of behaviors beyond explicitly forbidding any forms of dominance? They can and should test their own assumptions about the competencies of all members of the workforce because negative assumptions are often unconsciously communicated in powerful—albeit nonverbal—ways. For example, senior managers at Delta Manufacturing had for years allowed productivity and quality at their inner city plants to lag well behind the levels of other plants. When the company's chief executive officer began to question why the problem was never addressed, he came to realize that, in his heart, he had believed that inner-city workers, most of whom were African American or Hispanic, were not capable of doing better than subpar. In the end, the CEO and his senior management team were able to reverse their reasoning and take responsibility for improving the situation. The result was a sharp increase in the performance of the inner-city plants and a message to the entire organization about the capabilities of its entire workforce.

At Mastiff, the insurance company discussed earlier, the vice president and her manager decided to work with the recently promoted African American woman rather than demote her. They realized that their unit was really a pocket inside the larger organization: they did not have to wait for the rest of the organization to make a paradigm shift in order for their particular unit to change. So they met again to think about how to create conditions within their unit that would move the woman toward seeing her leadership position as encompassing all her skills. They assured her that her authentic style of leadership was precisely what they wanted her to bring to the job. They wanted her to be able to use whatever aspects of herself she thought would make her more effective in her work because the whole purpose was to do the job effectively, not to fit some preset traditional formula of how to behave. They let her know that, as a management team, they would try to adjust and change and support her. And they would deal with whatever consequences resulted from her exercising her decision rights in new ways.

Another example of this line of action—working against forms of dominance and subordination to enable full contribution—is the way the CEO of a major chemical company modified the attendance rules for his company's annual strategy conference. In the past, the conference had been attended only by senior executives, a relatively homogeneous group of white men. The company had been working hard on increasing the representation of women and people of color in its ranks, and the CEO could have left it at that. But he reckoned that, unless steps were taken, it would be ten years before the conferences tapped into the insights and perspectives of his newly diverse workforce. So he took the bold step of opening the conference to people from across all levels of the hierarchy, bringing together a diagonal slice of the organization. He also asked the conference organizers to come up with specific interventions, such as small group meetings before the larger session, to ensure that the new attendees would be comfortable enough to enter discussions. The result was that strategy-conference participants heard a much broader, richer, and livelier discussion about future scenarios for the company.

THEY ARE MAKING SURE THAT ORGANIZATIONAL TRUST STAYS INTACT

Few things are faster at killing a shift to a new way of thinking about diversity than feelings of broken trust. Therefore, managers of organizations that are successfully shifting to the learning-and-effectiveness paradigm take one more step: they make sure their organizations remain "safe" places for employees to be themselves. These managers recognize that tensions naturally arise as an organization begins to make room for diversity, starts to experiment with process and product ideas, and learns to reappraise its mission in light of suggestions from newly empowered constituents in the company. But as people put more of themselves out and open up about new feelings and ideas, the dynamics of the learning-and-effectiveness paradigm can produce temporary vulnerabilities. Managers who have helped their organizations make the change successfully have consistently demonstrated their commitment to the process and to all employees by setting a tone of honest discourse, by acknowledging tensions, and by resolving them sensitively and swiftly.

Our research over the past six years indicates that one cardinal limitation is at the root of companies' inability to attain the expected performance benefits of higher levels of diversity: the leadership's vision of the purpose of a diversified workforce. We have described the two most dominant orientations toward diversity and some of their consequences and limitations, together with a new framework for understanding and managing diversity. The learning-and-effectiveness paradigm we have outlined here is, undoubtedly, still in an emergent phase in those few organizations that embody it. We expect that as more organizations take on the challenge of truly engaging their diversity, new and unforeseen dilemmas will arise. Thus, perhaps more than anything else, a shift toward this paradigm requires a high-level commitment to learning more about the environment, structure, and tasks of one's organization, and giving improvement-generating change greater priority than the security of what is familiar. This is not an easy challenge, but we remain convinced that unless organizations take this step, any diversity initiative will fall short of fulfilling its rich promise.

The Research

THIS ARTICLE IS BASED ON a three-part research effort that began in 1990. Our subject was diversity; but, more specifically, we sought to understand three management challenges under that heading. First, how do organizations successfully achieve and sustain racial and gender diversity in their executive and middle-management ranks? Second, what is the impact of diversity on an organization's practices, processes, and performance? And, finally, how do leaders influence whether diversity becomes an enhancing or detracting element in the organization?

Over the following six years, we worked particularly closely with three organizations that had attained a high degree of demographic diversity: a small urban law firm, a community bank, and a 200-person consulting firm. In addition, we studied nine other companies in varying stages of diversifying their workforces. The group included two financial-services firms, three *Fortune* 500 manufacturing companies, two midsize high-technology companies, a private foundation, and a university medical center. In each case, we based our analysis on interviews, surveys, archival data, and observation. It is from this work that the third paradigm for managing diversity emerged and with it our belief that old and limiting assumptions about the meaning of diversity must be abandoned before its true potential can be realized as a powerful way to increase organizational effectiveness.

Originally published in September–October 1996
Reprint 96510

Women as a Business Imperative

FELICE N. SCHWARTZ

Executive Summary

IN 1989, Felice N. Schwartz's HBR article "Management Women and the New Facts of Life" generated a huge debate over the rules established by corporations in their handling of women executives. Now in "Women as a Business Imperative," Schwartz follows up with practical insights about the costs companies incur in passing over qualified businesswomen.

In the form of a memo to a fictional CEO, Schwartz describes how the atmosphere within most companies is corrosive to women and must change. Preconceptions harbored by male senior managers about women are so deeply ingrained that many men are not even aware of them. Yet senior managers must help women advance. Those companies that accept their responsibility to make radical change—both in women's treatment and in family support—can improve their bottom lines enormously.

Treating women as a business imperative is the equivalent of creating a unique R&D product for which there is great demand.

Most companies ignore child care and other family concerns. Many companies hire women to ensure mere adequacy and avoid litigation. Women's ambitions and energies are stifled by such businesses at the same time that women have demonstrated their competence and potential in the best business schools. High turnover results.

However, the restraints that now hold women back can be loosened easily. CEOs and other senior managers must support their female employees by (1) acknowledging the fundamental difference between women and men—the biological fact of maternity; (2) allowing flexibility for women and men who need it; (3) providing training that takes advantage of women's leadership potential; and (4) eliminating the corrosive atmosphere and the barriers that exist for women in the workplace.

Memo to: Peter Anderson

President, Chairman, and Chief Executive Officer

Topform Corporation

From: Felice N. Schwartz, President, Catalyst

Re: Women as a Business Imperative

A year ago, you asked me to analyze how Topform deals with its women and to advise you about your policies. Since then I have studied your company and talked at length with your top managers in order to arrive at a clear understanding of Topform's treatment of women.

You believe, I know, that you have made strides toward offering women equal opportunity. However, you think your efforts haven't been appreciated. The women who stand to profit most from your help don't seem grateful. You worry about the perplexingly high turnover of women within your managerial ranks, but, at the same time, you express annoyance at the messy details of modern double-gender business life, such as maternity leave and sexual harassment in the workplace. These problems seem distracting at best and, at worst, are obstacles to accomplishing your most important objectives: to make better products and to run a more profitable company.

Even though you value candor, you won't like what you're about to hear. If you are like most CEOs, you will want me to say that everything is all right, that the policies you've implemented have already made yours a family-friendly company. You will receive no such reassurances. In fact, my view is virtually the opposite: you must make a radical change now, not take more incremental, ad hoc steps. I must challenge you, not reassure you.

It is imperative that you help women advance in your company—and not just for their sake but for the sake of Topform as well. Moreover, the atmosphere of your company, which you regard as tolerant and welcoming to all employees, is actually corrosive to women. But if you accept this challenge and make a radical change in your treatment of women, you can effect tremendous improvement in your bottom line.

You and your peers who lead the most powerful companies in the United States are missing a huge opportunity. In fact, because you fundamentally misunderstand how to manage and motivate one-half of your human resources, you tap only a fraction of their capacity. One reason you continue to ignore these problems is that a conspiracy of silence precludes discussing the matter openly. You don't voice your concerns for fear of litigation, and you are joined in this conspiracy of silence by women who don't want to be seen as different from men. You pretend that everything is all right. But you cannot fix a problem that you tacitly avoid talking about.

Your company is not alone. Women encounter unpleasant, even harsh circumstances at *most* companies in our nation, even if CEOs and managers consider themselves enlightened, thoughtful, and compassionate people. Actually, Topform is better than many other companies. But the fact that you are neither alone nor the worst offender should not console you. You still need to change.

The solution is not merely instituting some "feel good" policies. The solution is fundamental change. It is a revolution in thought and action that will have a terrific impact, an impact that can be measured in dollars and cents.

What, for example, might be the economic power of this radical policy change? Imagine for a moment that you were not considering human resources policies but were instead attending a presentation from your R&D shop about a spectacular new product. This product, which has been under development for years, is now nearing completion. If its introduction succeeds—and you believe that it will—your revenues will skyrocket.

Wouldn't you react impatiently after that meeting ended, eager to get cracking? *Treating women as a business imperative is the equivalent of a unique R&D product for which there is a huge demand.* It promises to be the most important "new product launch" you and your company could implement. Making a radical change and accepting the women's imperative is the right thing to do; but, more important, it makes good economic sense.

U.S. Companies: From Zero to Five

You asked me to evaluate Topform. As you know, I travel all over the country, visiting and discussing these issues with hundreds of top executives yearly. These site visits and discussions have given me an empirical basis for comparing your company with many others.

From your vice president of human resources, I learned that almost half of all Topform employees are women. In fact, 40% of your exempt employees and 7% of your vice presidents are female. These percentages compare favorably with national averages. But simply counting women employees, vice presidents, or board members is not an effective way to appraise corporate performance. Both of us realize that setting arbitrary numerical objectives can produce spurious accounting, which in turn produces false reassurances, while chronic underlying problems go unaddressed. Attempting to measure complicated personnel questions by using only the blunt instrument of the adding machine is a mistake. As subtle as these issues are, and as difficult as it may be to translate them into cold mathematics, it helps nonetheless to look at them critically. Consequently, I have developed a simple but effective rating system that runs from zero to five to gauge how motivated companies are to accept the women's imperative as a *business* imperative.

At the low end, *Zeros* are companies that are dead to the issue of developing women. They simply don't care. These companies make no effort to recruit, train, or promote women. Executives at Zero companies work with blinders on. They are even blase about the law. They get sued, repeatedly in some cases, but apparently accept the costs of settling those suits as just another annoying part of doing business—their way.

Next are the companies that simply want to keep ahead of the law. They are *Ones*. They track numbers and fill out Equal Employment Opportunity Commission forms, but they don't take any initiative in leveling the playing field for women or addressing the needs of working parents, which are still, unfortunately, the needs of working women. According to one study, for instance, a third of U.S. companies have done virtually nothing that is not legally mandated to help their employees cope with family problems. By my standards, those companies are Ones.

Twos are companies that want to do what is fair and right. The Twos have formulated two or three specific policies for child care, part-time clerical jobs, or unpaid maternity leave—but those who work at the company still feel it is a man's world. Twos give little thought to women's upward mobility or to removing the obstacles to women's productivity. Deep down, the men who run these companies believe that women should not be part of the real action. They go through the motions of improving women's situations, but they have not come to terms with their deeply rooted preconceptions.

There are only a few employers who can legitimately say, "We are doing well by women," even in a limited sense, on family and work issues or leadership development. Those companies that do I call *Threes.* For example, newspaper giant Gannett, where there is a passion to develop women, is a Three. (In fact, the former publisher of Gannett's successful *USA Today,* Cathleen Black, is a woman.) The Federal National Mortgage Association, which increased the number of women employees from 4% in 1981 to 26% in 1988, is another Three. IBM, which built on Thomas Watson's respect for the individual, and Corning, which has a strategic plan for change, are both Threes.

Fours are mythical companies where one day the playing field will be leveled for everyone. No one is there yet, but some companies such as Xerox are at least trying to get there. Companies at the Four level would be truly responsive to women. These would be companies managed by men and women who have examined their own preconceptions and shaken off those vestiges of old-fashioned, outdated thinking that prevent progress.

Fives are off today's charts. The Five level is a place where the playing field itself starts off flat for both men and women. This exemplary vision includes an ideal, egalitarian environment, where the whole management structure is not a power-oriented hierarchy of ascending status at all but a jungle gym with lateral sidebars and many-leveled challenges, with help and rewards available for employees at every step. Becoming a Five will represent the ultimate achievement, and it will yield the ultimate payoff.

Right now, most companies stand at levels One or Two. Their executives ardently believe that they are "OK on women," that the policies they've adopted are appropriately enlightened. Of course, they don't think they are on the cutting edge—but, then again, they don't want to be ahead of the curve.

They are complacent—and they are in danger.

Your company, like many others, is stuck at Two.

Eight Costs of Where Women Are

Here is another way to view the problem. Imagine that your corporate management group takes the form of a pyramid. (Whether or not Topform's structure should be a pyramid or a different shape is an interesting question by itself but not one we will discuss at the moment.) In 1960, virtually all of the white-collar employees in your company—and in the management ranks of almost all companies in the United States—were men. Today more than a third of your managers—370 out of 1,000—are women. That represents improvement.

This improvement was almost inevitable, of course, given the changing demographics of the country. There simply are not enough capable men available today to fill all of the managerial jobs. Your human resources director can tell you that the nation's labor pool isn't growing fast enough to keep up with management demand. Family size contracted from an average of almost four children per family in the 1950s to fewer than two children per family from the mid-1970s to today. The new generation of college graduates—52% female—from which you recruit your future managers is much smaller than anticipated. This age group is actually only half the expected size based on demographic predictions that assumed the baby boom would continue.

Of course, the current downturn, as well as mergers, restructurings, and job consolidations, has had a crushing impact on the lives of those managers who have lost their jobs. This pain and despair is experienced by both men and women. We should acknowledge and sympathize with those who are suffering. However, this dismal period will end, and we must regain our competitive position in the world economy. To do so, we must mobilize our talent. Women are not part of the problem, they are part of the solution.

There are already women executives today throughout U.S. business. As a matter of fact, about 37% of your managers are women. That's progress, of a sort. But consider where most of these women are: in jobs at the bottom of your team's pyramid.

Picture the company pyramid in your mind's eye again. It is a geometric truth that if you divide any pyramid into four slices of equal height, the top slice will contain 1.5% of its volume, the next slice will contain 11%, the third slice will contain 29.5%, and the bottom layer will contain 58%.

Now note that out of 1,000 managers at Topform, 15 are in the pyramid's top slice, the corporate pinnacle where all of your other ambitious staffers set their sights. In the second slice are 110 of your managers, with 295 on the third level, and 580 on the bottom. The pyramid's bottom slice contains the entry-level management jobs where promising junior people as well as competent but unexceptional older managers are found.

When we analyze where Topform's women are, we find that their distribution is typical of the pattern for Two companies in the United States. Half of your entry-level managers on the lowest level are women. Fewer than one-quarter of the jobs in the next level up are held by women. Of the managers on the second tier, only 10% are women. And only 1 of your 15 highest ranking managers is a woman.

What is wrong with this picture? Over the last decade, you have led an effort to recruit bright, promising men and women to join Topform's management ranks, as most U.S. companies have done. You have searched for talent in the best undergraduate and business schools in the land, schools in which there are more women in attendance every year. You yourself have told me that the women at Topform are as strong in basic leadership traits like intelligence, energy, and analytical ability as the men because your standards are exacting and you expect to hire only the best people. And yet women languish after you hire them.

If women are as smart, capable, and eager to exercise their skills as men are, all of which you say you believe, then why are the highest two levels in your company almost exclusively male domains? Ignore the matter of what is right or wrong. What does that segregation, intended or not, cost you? How are you hurt?

1. **You're not mobilizing your best people at the top.**
   Any successful business today is only as good as its senior management team. Traditionally, the most prestigious corporations (like yours) and the top professional companies have confined their hiring to the top 10% of potential management employees. In the past, that meant selective recruiting of the highest ranked available men who could be found at elite business schools. However, today women have displaced men in these schools. Women now earn 55% of all undergraduate accounting degrees and 35% of

MBAs. So if you attempt to depend solely on male graduates from the top 10% of the best schools in the country, you will drastically reduce the pool from which you draw.

2. **You're not maintaining quality at every level.** Today the marketplace offers little leeway for managerial error. The nation's leadership needs are growing rapidly both in quantity and in quality—and doing so faster than the work force itself is growing. Competition has become global and more intense. International corporations vie with one another in every sizable industry and in every market that offers promise. Products grow more sophisticated each day. Technology grows more complex. Managers have to be very, very good.

   Now that a significant number of women are in management, you can concentrate on enhancing the quality of your people at every level by identifying and promoting the best women instead of benignly ignoring them after you hire them. In fact, one of the United States's greatest assets in international competition is its pool of qualified female managers. Recognition of the contribution that U.S. women can make to business success, whatever this country's current shortcomings, gives the United States a terrific advantage in competing against some of its toughest competitors like Japan. In that nation, women have barely gained token entrée into lower management circles. Japanese salarymen already seem to be working at peak capacity, which leaves little room for ratcheting up the intensity they already bring to their jobs.

Thank goodness women are available for consideration as part of the talent pool in the United States.
But unless you actively draw from the entire universe
of people with high potential, *including* women candidates, you will hurt your company and yourself. If
you fail to draw, train, and advance women candidates, you will neither hone this national advantage,
nor will you compete successfully in the United
States or beyond.

3. **You're treating a big portion of your employees as
   dead weight.** There is a psychological lag between
   Topform's decision to employ women and your will
   to use them. You accept women as workers, but in
   your mind, they really have not entered the mainstream of business. Not only are most of the women
   in your managerial ranks situated at the bottom of
   the pyramid but they have also been shunted off to
   the sides. In your mind, women are ancillary. Is it
   possible that you still think as bosses did 30 years
   ago? Do you secretly think that men belong in business, while women create problems? Are you hiring,
   training, and advancing women only to ensure mere
   adequacy? Does adequate female managerial representation mean doing just enough to quell women's
   restlessness, avoid the wrath and litigation of women
   employees, satisfy the corporate conscience, and
   develop a few high performers for show? Do you pay
   lip service to equality between the sexes while
   unconsciously sabotaging that equality?

   If nearly half of your managers are women who are
   discounted in this way, then you're dragging a very
   heavy anchor.

4. **You're putting a lid on the contribution individual women can make.** You stifle people when you make them report to less talented bosses. Many female managers, who occupy the sides and bottom of the organizational chart, are working for men who are less talented than they are. Thus their talent and vision are constrained by the limitations of the underqualified men to whom they report.

A person who works for someone less competent is stunted and thwarted by that relationship. The capable but underappreciated subordinate soon realizes that recognition for effort is not commensurate with output and that the rewards of her work are not sufficient. It is enervating to work for a boss whom one does not respect. The results are predictable: the more talented subordinate throttles down, begins to cut back, produces less, or leaves altogether.

Inequity and injustice of this kind have real fiscal costs. The company suffers from decreased productivity and inefficiency. These problems are compounded when they are systemic; for instance, when it is clear to all of the women managers in an organization that women are victimized by consistently insensitive treatment and by relegation to second-class managerial citizenship. Add to this already punishing environment the effects of inadvertent sexist behavior. To be sure, not all sexist behavior is overt, such as a pinch at the watercooler, an off-color joke that is intended to throw the woman who hears it off-guard, or much worse, pernicious sexual harassment. Some of it is tacit, unspoken, and attitudinal. Most of it is unconscious. Regardless, for many women, working means encountering a series of hurdles and tests. The problem is exacerbated at the upper levels of the company hierarchy, where negative experiences become more intense because women are fewer and more isolated.

With each step backward, women are further debilitated, and attrition among your highest potential women increases. This may, in fact, explain the relative overrepresentation of talented women entrepreneurs. Some of the best women set out to work for themselves in a supportive environment of their own creation where talent can be recognized and rewarded.

5. **You're undervaluing promising people who wish to take a role in family caregiving.** Very simply, if you see commitment to your company as the inverse of employees' commitment to their families, you're creating a false and damaging dichotomy for judging employee potential. Worse, this division of commitments perpetuates the prejudice that it is not possible to combine career and family. As a consequence, business loses good people who would bring the same high standards to their work that they bring to their families—if given the choice *not* to make a choice between work and home.

It is almost second nature to think of child and elder care as "women's work," domestic issues, matters that have nothing to do with the rough-and-tumble business world. Revenues, margins, rates of return, market share—these are supposed to be the primary

concerns of business. Making things and selling
things are business concerns. But rearing children is
a women's issue. Because women haven't been
assimilated fully into business, child care isn't considered a business issue, nor is flexibility thought to
be an important company priority.

No one can deny that since women have entered the
nation's work force in vast numbers, there is no
longer a solid family-support structure at home. Only
16% of full-time workers go home to a non-working
spouse, according to the Bureau of Labor Statistics.
In two-career couples, neither parent can expect that
the other will automatically tend to the needs of their
children. Since high-quality, affordable day care is
rare, many working parents are permanently anxious
about their children. And as the population ages,
these working parents are often responsible for their
own elderly parents too.

But the clock will not go backward. If all of the
United States's working women were to return home
to cook and clean tomorrow, businesses would disin-
tegrate. U.S. business depends on women. Companies may not use them as well as they should, but
they depend on women employees no less.

The result? When companies don't offer child care
and flexibility in scheduling work as matters of
course, these companies suffer along with their
deprived workers. And those individuals who drop
out may be some of the most responsible employees,
those in the company who could bring the same
uncompromising standards to their performance in

the workplace that they do to the rearing of their children.

6. **You're wasting recruiting and training money.** On average, college-educated women postpone the birth of their first child until they are 31 years old. If a woman joins your company after her college graduation, Topform makes a decade-long commitment to her training and development. If she leaves you when her child is born—because your culture retards her career growth, or because parental-leave provisions and family support are inadequate—you fail to amortize that ten-year investment. It is worse for you, of course, if she leaves Topform to work for a competitor and puts her experience to work against you. Ironically, wherever she goes, the unhappy cycle continues because chances are good you'll replace her with another woman who may not work out at all and will in any case need training and development for years before she (or a male counterpart, for that matter) can perform on par with the original woman you lost. Then, when the replacement has a baby— which is also probable—the whole cycle begins again.

7. **You're failing to create beacons for the best women entering the workplace.** You know that women constitute an increasing proportion of a shrinking work force, and you believe that Topform needs all the help it can get. But do you view hiring women as a last resort? If so, that is shortsighted.

Companies that do not take pains to develop and retain able women will continue to feel the absence of women at higher levels in the future, when all talent will be scarcer. The smartest women graduating from the best schools will scout out their employment prospects, searching for the right beacons. They will conclude, reasonably enough, that companies that advance few women to the upper tiers are less attractive than those that have already demonstrated they value women. Companies that fail to develop women for leadership positions now will be forced to settle later for women who are not as qualified. Nonetheless, half of your management pyramid will be women in the future. If you attract only those women who are second tier, you will lose a competitive advantage.

8. **You could be capitalizing on a tremendous opportunity.** Women can lead your company to new profitability.

When you expand the pool from which you draw your top management, you will see greater talent at every level of the enterprise. In an information economy, an economy of ideas, an economy of knowledge, nothing is more important than the thinking skills of your people and their capacity to make smart, timely decisions. Better decisions lead to enhanced productivity, improved pricing and packaging, and more ingenious innovations. You need to attract—and win—the commitment of managers with those skills. The best way to win their commitment to Topform is to demonstrate your commitment to them. You can earn the loyalty of the women in your organization at a time when loyalty is a vanishing U.S. corporate virtue. By providing flexibility, you will retain good women through the childbearing years just as they become most useful to the company. And a solid cadre of women at the senior levels will serve as role models and mentors to junior women as they rise.

This new approach will appeal to your stockholders, more than half of whom are women, both for economic reasons and reasons of principle. Your public image will improve, which is not an insignificant issue. Today companies compete through their values as well as their products. Customers want to know what a company stands for. When a company can demonstrate that it has moved aggressively in the way in which it recruits, trains, promotes, rewards, and values women, it will not only attract the brightest women, it will speak directly to the millions of women and men who care deeply about this issue. A company's reputation for good human values is as valuable an asset as capital equipment. When your customers, clients, and employees realize that you value women as a central resource rather than inadvertently perpetuating a system that defeats them, a new, positive cycle will be born to replace the old, unhappy, expensive one.

Women are not going to go home again. The clock ticks forward, not back. So you can either force women and men who wish to participate in family life to make some very unpleasant choices, or you and your company can change. You can insist that women play by men's rules, and as a result, they will fail. Similarly, you can insist that men follow in their father's footsteps and focus their energies on careers, limiting severely their participation in their children's lives. You can require women and men to give up the dream of having children. Or you can urge those who have children to turn them over to full-time surrogate care. And some of your employees will leave Topform to work elsewhere or to start businesses of their own that give them more flexibility and career satisfaction.

Or you can do everything possible to support families while clearing away the barriers to women's—and men's—progress.

Four Actions for Change

The biggest obstacle to corporate change is the reluctance of leaders to see the need for it. When you accept the notion that women should be full participants in the management of your company, when you are ready to consider changing, you'll find that implementing a solution is neither difficult nor expensive. *The restraints that now hold women back can be loosened easily, and these problems will be swiftly remedied.*

There are four actions you should take to ensure that the women you employ will function as effectively as the men. The first is to acknowledge the fundamental difference between women and men, the biological fact of maternity. The second is to provide flexibility for women and men who want it. Third is to provide women who already have basic leadership traits with the special additional management skills and tools that are vital to excellent performance. The last action you can take is to improve the corporate environment by removing barriers that exist for women but not for men.

ACKNOWLEDGE MATERNITY

End the conspiracy of silence in which leaders as well as workers pretend that they think the biological differences between the sexes do not exist. Of all women, 85%

have babies. Giving birth is a uniquely female experience. These are facts. But they are facts that companies don't handle well.

We should distinguish pregnancy, childbirth, and disability from parenting. Maternity, when defined as childbearing, is predictable and finite. It is good practical policy to acknowledge this natural process and to help women as they move through it. You can manage maternity so that it takes a small fraction of current costs in productivity and attrition.

There's no denying the physical and emotional impact of pregnancy. Yet most women find pregnancy an experience of heightened energy and happy anticipation. Within the last few decades, the average woman has changed her pattern from one of leaving work at the end of the first trimester to working right up until the month, if not the week or day, of delivery. What discourages pregnant women are the attitudes of other people in the workplace. The supervisor and colleagues of the mother-to-be tend to discount her and see her condition as something negative rather than the plus it is. At best today, a pregnant woman's condition is ignored. At worst, she is forced to hide her pregnancy as long as possible and to avoid natural coping responses such as walking around at intervals during long meetings, elevating her feet when seated, or wearing comfortable clothes.

You should formulate clear, comprehensive disability and maternity-leave policies—as differentiated from a parental-leave policy—that will enable you to retain your best women. Do not require an unequivocal statement of intentions from the mother-to-be before the baby is born. Wise, self-interested companies will allow women to return to work when they are ready, when child-care arrangements are in place, and permit those women to have flexible schedules that will help them be productive. It is my belief that most women will opt to return early on part-time schedules. Thus paid maternity leave is not an issue—and a modest fraction of the expense of that forgone paid leave could be used to subsidize the part-time return of low-income women.

Finally, work coverage when the woman is on leave must be jointly planned by both the employee and her manager. Encourage frank talk. When you help women employees with maternity rather than punish them, you'll inspire their confidence and be rewarded with candor that permits you to plan accordingly. The fact that women have babies doesn't alter their commitment to a job or the quality of their work—except when maternity goes unacknowledged, unplanned for, and unmanaged.

PROVIDE FLEXIBILITY

Begin by accepting that parenthood is linked to business and that intact families include two parents. Note that there is no evidence that men are less nurturing than women. Just a few years ago, talk of "co-parenting" would have taxed the patience of male senior managers, so advocates of shared parental responsibility had to tackle maternity first. Now we can talk openly.

A small percentage of men *and* women are singularly career-focused, while a small number are entirely family-focused. But the vast majority of men and women want to co_____ch their_____ugh-out t_____d women require flexibility in order to be productive at work and to be active, responsible parents.

Now that women are in the work force, children have a business impact. Today you must accept parenthood as a part of doing business. You can reduce its cost by consciously disregarding the traditional roles of men and women. The result will be that you, the employer, will get the best, most committed workers and that children will get the best, most committed parents. Moreover, the net return to the employer when husbands and wives share parenting will be greater. When women are forced to be primary caregivers, their productivity and their careers become stunted because they cannot come to work early or stay late. However, when parenting is shared, either parent can be home with the children and both parents are free to make a serious, sustained commitment to their employers, their careers, and their children.

Permit parents to cut back to half-time (at prorated pay) and then reenter the competition for senior management jobs, partnerships, or tenure if they choose. Let new fathers take paternity leaves in sequence with their wives. Encourage and legitimize the growing desire of men to take an active role in parenting. Since some women choose to spend five or six years with young children, don't shoot yourself in the foot by denying them reentry and the chance to move up when they return. It is crusty tradition that makes us think that the thirties are the prime career years. When these women return refreshed, guilt-free, and ready to go at full throttle, they can produce for 25 or 30 more strong years.

Let parents (and other executives) work at home. New technology—personal computers, fax machines, modems, and so on—makes working at home practical.

Take advantage of the freedom this technology affords. And, finally, learn how to measure real *productivity* instead of counting hours spent in the office.

PROVIDE TRAINING

Helping women maximize their potential helps not only them but also your company. You recruit only the best managerial candidates, good men and women, from a pool that is both diminishing in total number and increasingly female (51% of all master's degrees, for instance, now go to women). But don't stop at simply avoiding discrimination in hiring. Recognize that women face a tougher challenge than men do after they join your male-oriented company.

Women are newcomers to the male world of business. Their socialization does not prepare them for this new world. Some men view them as temporary, uninvited guests whom they treat insensitively and accept grudgingly, if at all. Often women are penalized for lacking aggressive instincts, but, contradictorily, they are scorned for being too aggressive. So you must help your promising women with training and education that includes behavioral advice. Permit them to display the qualities that are traditionally inculcated in men: competitiveness, aggressiveness, risk-taking, and long-term, dependable commitment to a career.

Fortunately for women, the work world has become increasingly information-oriented, which means that supposedly innate feminine skills in communication and sensitivity are at a premium. But if you need managers to act authoritatively, give women permission to be as tough and aggressive as you need them to be; you'll find they respond accordingly. Watch women managers grow after they become comfortable in the workplace.

IMPROVE THE ENVIRONMENT

Removing the barriers that obstruct women entails first accepting the premise that women belong in the work force—and then eliminating the corrosive atmosphere that pervades most companies. The glass ceiling is not a physical barrier erected by nefarious CEOs. Rather, it is an attitudinal hurdle consisting of largely unconscious stereotypes and preconceptions. So make men aware of negative behavior. Sensitize your male managers to the new demographic realities and the practical reasons for proper conduct between the sexes at work. Eradicate sexual harassment.

Next, coach women as you do men, and accept in women the behavior that usually characterizes successful men. Assign them to line jobs that will tax and teach them. At the same time, don't feel betrayed when women plateau or drop out; instead, ask yourself whether conditions in your company forced them out. And don't worry about raising women's expectations too much by announcing your intention to change. If you don't raise expectations, women will despair that the status quo will never change.

My hope is that Topform and all U.S. companies will work to integrate the lives of their employees, permitting work and family to fit smoothly together instead of conflicting with one another. When work supplies energy to the home, and home revitalizes life on the job, each half joins to make a vibrant whole. If, on the other hand, the status quo does not change, bitterness and frustration will grow.

Can we achieve this ideal? We have come so far since the revolution began 30 years ago, when women began pouring into the work force. Further movement, accelerated movement, is not only logical but also eminently practical.

But it is not inevitable. If the status quo goes unchallenged, many more women will leave corporations and professions to become entrepreneurs. Men who remain at these corporations will be forced to work harder. They will suffer from fatigue, frustration, diminished productivity, and further estrangement from their families. The women who continue working and remain primarily responsible for home management and child care won't be able to compete for leadership positions.

Most likely, if unchallenged, the pace of change will be just fast enough to perpetuate the conspiracy of silence. In that case, we'll remain where we are now, where it is not working. Everybody knows it, but nobody is talking about it.

I believe the process of change must begin with CEOs who now cling to an image of the past that tells them women should be home rearing children. They think women's careers burn out prematurely because work is not really as important to them as it is to men. They believe there always will be enough high-performing males to replenish their ranks.

But CEOs will change because business is quintessentially realistic. Senior executives will see the many changes in the workplace that have already succeeded and the many changes that are still necessary. And they will cast aside their stereotypes and preconceptions.

The logjam impeding women's forward movement will be broken by a top-level acknowledgment that the status quo is unacceptable. As this movement accelerates, we should see more women and men break with traditional sex roles. We should see more self-determinate women. Men will grow more comfortable inside the home, and this too will have positive ramifications. Couples may be able to build partnerships that preclude feelings of exploitation and anger. Families will grow stronger.

But the best news I can offer is this prediction: your company will gain tremendous financial benefits when you accept your responsibility to women and working parents.

Originally published in March–April 1992
Reprint 92207

Ways Women Lead

JUDY B. ROSENER

Executive Summary

WOMEN MANAGERS ARE SUCCEEDING not by adopting the traditional command-and-control leadership style but by drawing on what is unique to their experience as women. According to a study the author conducted for the International Women's Forum, men and women in similar managerial jobs make the same amount of money and experience roughly the same degree of work-family conflict. But when they describe their leadership styles, vast differences arise.

Men are much more likely than women to view leadership as a series of transactions with subordinates, and to use their position and control of resources to motivate their followers. Women, on the other hand, are far more likely than men to describe themselves as transforming subordinates' self-interest into concern for the whole organization and as using personal traits like charisma, work record, and interpersonal skills to motivate others.

Women leaders practice what the author calls "interactive leadership"—trying to make every interaction with coworkers positive for all involved by encouraging participation, sharing power and information, making people feel important, and energizing them.

In general, women have been expected to be supportive and cooperative, and they have not held long series of positions with formal authority. This may explain why women leaders today tend to be more interactive than men. But interactive leadership should not be linked directly to being female, since some men use that style and some women prefer the command-and-control style. Organizations that are open to leadership styles that play to individuals' strengths will increase their chances of surviving in a fast-changing environment.

WOMEN MANAGERS WHO HAVE broken the glass ceiling in medium-sized, nontraditional organizations have proven that effective leaders don't come from one mold. They have demonstrated that using the command-and-control style of managing others, a style generally associated with men in large, traditional organizations, is not the only way to succeed.

The first female executives, because they were breaking new ground, adhered to many of the "rules of conduct" that spelled success for men. Now a second wave of women is making its way into top management, not by adopting the style and habits that have proved successful for men but by drawing on the skills and attitudes they developed from their shared experience as women. These

second-generation managerial women are drawing on
what is unique to their socialization as women and creating a different path to the top. They are seeking and
finding opportunities in fast-changing and growing organizations to show that they can achieve results—in a different way. They are succeeding because of—not in spite
of—certain characteristics generally considered to be
"feminine" and inappropriate in leaders.

The women's success shows that a nontraditional
leadership style is well suited to the conditions of some
work environments and can increase an organization's
chances of surviving in an uncertain world. It supports
the belief that there is strength in a diversity of leadership styles.

In a recent survey sponsored by the International
Women's Forum, I found a number of unexpected similarities between men and women leaders along with
some important differences. (For more on the study and
its findings, see "The IWF Survey of Men and Women
Leaders.") Among these similarities are characteristics
related to money and children. I found that the men and
women respondents earned the same amount of money
(and the household income of the women is twice that of
the men). This finding is contrary to most studies, which
find a considerable wage gap between men and women,
even at the executive level. I also found that just as many
men as women experience work-family conflict
(although when there are children at home, the women
experience slightly more conflict than men).

But the similarities end when men and women
describe their leadership performance and how they usually influence those with whom they work. The men are
more likely than the women to describe themselves in
ways that characterize what some management experts

call "transactional" leadership.[1] That is, they view job performance as a series of transactions with subordinates—exchanging rewards for services rendered or punishment for inadequate performance. The men are also more likely to use power that comes from their organizational position and formal authority.

The women respondents, on the other hand, described themselves in ways that characterize "transformational" leadership—getting subordinates to transform their own self-interest into the interest of the group through concern for a broader goal. Moreover, they ascribe their power to personal characteristics like charisma, interpersonal skills, hard work, or personal contacts rather than to organizational stature.

Intrigued by these differences, I interviewed some of the women respondents who described themselves as transformational. These discussions gave me a better picture of how these women view themselves as leaders and a greater understanding of the important ways in which their leadership style differs from the traditional command-and-control style. I call their leadership style "interactive leadership" because these women actively work to make their interactions with subordinates positive for everyone involved. More specifically, the women encourage participation, share power and information, enhance other people's self-worth, and get others excited about their work. All these things reflect their belief that allowing employees to contribute and to feel powerful and important is a win-win situation—good for the employees and the organization.

Interactive Leadership

From my discussions with the women interviewees, several patterns emerged. The women leaders made frequent reference to their efforts to encourage participation and share power and information—two things that are often associated with participative management. But their self-description went beyond the usual definitions of participation. Much of what they described were attempts to enhance other people's sense of self-worth and to energize followers. In general, these leaders believe that people perform best when they feel good about themselves and their work, and they try to create situations that contribute to that feeling.

ENCOURAGE PARTICIPATION

Inclusion is at the core of interactive leadership. In describing nearly every aspect of management, the women interviewees made reference to trying to make people feel part of the organization. They try to instill this group identity in a variety of ways, including encouraging others to have a say in almost every aspect of work, from setting performance goals to determining strategy. To facilitate inclusion, they create mechanisms that get people to participate and they use a conversational style that sends signals inviting people to get involved.

One example of the kinds of mechanisms that encourage participation is the "bridge club" that one interviewee, a group executive in charge of mergers and acquisitions at a large East Coast financial firm, created. The club is an informal gathering of people who have information she needs but over whom she has no direct control. The word *bridge* describes the effort to bring together these "members" from different functions. The word *club* captures the relaxed atmosphere.

Despite the fact that attendance at club meetings is voluntary and over and above the usual work demands, the interviewee said that those whose help she needs make the time to come. "They know their contributions are valued, and they appreciate the chance to exchange information across functional boundaries in an informal setting that's fun." She finds participation in the club more effective than memos.

Whether or not the women create special forums for people to interact, they try to make people feel included as a matter of course, often by trying to draw them into the conversation or soliciting their opinions. Frieda Caplan, founder and CEO of Frieda's Finest, a California-based marketer and distributor of unusual fruits and vegetables, described an approach she uses that is typical of the other women interviewed: "When I face a tough decision, I always ask my employees, 'What would you do if you were me?' This approach generates good ideas and introduces my employees to the complexity of management decisions."

Of course, saying that you include others doesn't mean others necessarily feel included. The women acknowledge the possibility that their efforts to draw people in may be seen as symbolic, so they try to avoid that perception by acting on the input they receive. They ask for suggestions before they reach their own conclusions, and they test—and sometimes change—particular decisions before they implement them. These women use participation to clarify their own views by thinking things through out loud and to ensure that they haven't overlooked an important consideration.

The fact that many of the interviewees described their participatory style as coming "naturally" suggests that these leaders do not consciously adopt it for its business value. Yet they realize that encouraging participation has benefits. For one thing, making it easy for people to express their ideas helps ensure that decisions reflect as much information as possible. To some of the women, this point is just common sense. Susan S. Elliott, president and founder of Systems Service Enterprises, a St. Louis computer consulting company, expressed this view: "I can't come up with a plan and then ask those who manage the accounts to give me their reactions. They're the ones who really know the accounts. They have information I don't have. Without their input I'd be operating in an ivory tower."

Participation also increases support for decisions ultimately reached and reduces the risk that ideas will be undermined by unexpected opposition. Claire Rothman, general manager of the Great Western Forum, a large sports and entertainment arena in Los Angeles, spoke about the value of open disagreement: "When I know ahead of time that someone disagrees with a decision, I can work especially closely with that person to try to get his or her support."

Getting people involved also reduces the risk associated with having only one person handle a client, project, or investment. For Patricia M. Cloherty, senior vice president and general partner of Alan Patricof Associates, a New York venture capital firm, including people in decision making and planning gives investments longevity. If something happens to one person, others will be familiar enough with the situation to "adopt" the investment. That way, there are no orphans in the portfolio, and a knowledgeable second opinion is always available.

Like most who are familiar with participatory management, these women are aware that being inclusive also has its disadvantages. Soliciting ideas and information from others takes time, often requires giving up some control, opens the door to criticism, and exposes personal and turf conflicts. In addition, asking for ideas and information can be interpreted as not having answers.

Further, it cannot be assumed that everyone wants to participate. Some people prefer being told what to do. When Mary Jane Rynd was a partner in a Big Eight accounting firm in Arizona (she recently left to start her own company—Rynd, Carneal & Associates), she encountered such a person: "We hired this person from an out-of-state CPA firm because he was experienced and smart—and because it's always fun to hire someone away from another firm. But he was just too cynical to participate. He was suspicious of everybody. I tried everything to get him involved—including him in discussions and giving him pep talks about how we all work together. Nothing worked. He just didn't want to participate."

Like all those who responded to the survey, these women are comfortable using a variety of leadership styles. So when participation doesn't work, they act unilaterally. "I prefer participation," said Elliott, "but there are situations where time is short and I have to take the bull by the horns."

SHARE POWER AND INFORMATION

Soliciting input from other people suggests a flow of information from employees to the "boss." But part of making people feel included is knowing that open communication flows in two directions. These women say they willingly share power and information rather than guard it and they make apparent their reasoning behind decisions. While many leaders see information as power and power as a limited commodity to be coveted, the interviewees seem to be comfortable letting power and information change hands. As Adrienne Hall, vice chairman of Eisaman, Johns & Laws, a large West Coast advertising firm, said: "I know territories shift, so I'm not preoccupied with turf."

One example of power and information sharing is the open strategy sessions held by Debi Coleman, vice president of information systems and technology at Apple Computer. Rather than closeting a small group of key executives in her office to develop a strategy based on her own agenda, she holds a series of meetings over several days and allows a larger group to develop and help choose alternatives.

The interviewees believe that sharing power and information accomplishes several things. It creates loyalty by signaling to coworkers and subordinates that they are trusted and their ideas respected. It also sets an example for other people and therefore can enhance the general communication flow. And it increases the odds that leaders will hear about problems before they explode. Sharing power and information also gives employees and coworkers the wherewithal to reach conclusions, solve problems, and see the justification for decisions.

On a more pragmatic level, many employees have come to expect their bosses to be open and frank. They no longer accept being dictated to but want to be treated as individuals with minds of their own. As Elliott said, "I work with lots of people who are bright and intelligent, so I have to deal with them at an intellectual level. They're very logical, and they want to know the reasons for things. They'll buy in only if it makes sense."

In some cases, sharing information means simply being candid about work-related issues. In early 1990, when Elliott hired as employees many of the people she had been using as independent contractors, she knew the transition would be difficult for everyone. The number of employees nearly doubled overnight, and the nature of working relationships changed. "I warned everyone that we were in for some rough times and reminded them that we would be experiencing them together. I admitted that it would also be hard for me, and I made it clear that I wanted them to feel free to talk to me. I was completely candid and encouraged them to be honest with me. I lost some employees who didn't like the new relationships, but I'm convinced that being open helped me understand my employees better, and it gave them a feeling of support."

Like encouraging participation, sharing power and information has its risks. It allows for the possibility that people will reject, criticize, or otherwise challenge what the leader has to say or, more broadly, her authority. Also, employees get frustrated when leaders listen to— but ultimately reject—their ideas. Because information is a source of power, leaders who share it can be seen as naive or needing to be liked. The interviewees have experienced some of these downsides but find the positives overwhelming.

ENHANCE THE SELF-WORTH OF OTHERS

One of the by-products of sharing information and encouraging participation is that employees feel important. During the interviews, the women leaders discussed other ways they build a feeling of self-worth in co-workers and subordinates. They talked about giving others credit and praise and sending small signals of recognition. Most important, they expressed how they refrain from asserting their own superiority, which asserts the inferiority of others. All those I interviewed expressed clear aversion to behavior that sets them apart from others in the company—reserved parking places, separate dining facilities, pulling rank.

Examples of sharing and giving credit to others abound. Caplan, who has been the subject of scores of media reports hailing her innovation of labeling vegetables so consumers know what they are and how to cook them, originally got the idea from a farmer. She said that whenever someone raises the subject, she credits the farmer and downplays her role. Rothman is among the many note-writers: when someone does something out of the ordinary, she writes them a personal note to tell them she noticed. Like many of the women I interviewed, she said she also makes a point of acknowledging good work by talking about it in front of others.

Bolstering coworkers and subordinates is especially important in businesses and jobs that tend to be hard on a person's ego. Investment banking is one example because of the long hours, high pressures, intense competition, and inevitability that some deals will fail. One interviewee in investment banking hosts dinners for her division, gives out gag gifts as party favors, passes out M&Ms at meetings, and throws parties "to celebrate ourselves." These things, she said, balance the anxiety that permeates the environment.

Rynd compensates for the negativity inherent in preparing tax returns: "In my business we have something called a query sheet, where the person who reviews the tax return writes down everything that needs to be corrected. Criticism is built into the system. But at the end of every review, I always include a positive comment—your work paper technique looked good, I appreciate the fact that you got this done on time, or something like that. It seems trivial, but it's one way to remind people that I recognize their good work and not just their shortcomings."

ENERGIZE OTHERS

The women leaders spoke of their enthusiasm for work and how they spread their enthusiasm around to make work a challenge that is exhilarating and fun. The women leaders talked about it in those terms and claimed to use their enthusiasm to get others excited. As Rothman said, "There is rarely a person I can't motivate."

Enthusiasm was a dominant theme throughout the interviews. In computer consulting: "Because this business is on the forefront of technology, I'm sort of evangelistic about it, and I want other people to be as excited as I am." In venture capital: "You have to have a head of steam." In executive search: "Getting people excited is an important way to influence those you have no control over." Or in managing sports arenas: "My enthusiasm gets others excited. I infuse them with energy and make them see that even boring jobs contribute to the fun of working in a celebrity business."

Enthusiasm can sometimes be misunderstood. In conservative professions like investment banking, such an upbeat leadership style can be interpreted as cheerleading and can undermine credibility. In many cases, the women said they won and preserved their credibility by achieving results that could be measured easily. One of the women acknowledged that her colleagues don't understand or like her leadership style and have called it cheerleading. "But," she added, "in this business you get credibility from what you produce, and they love the profits I generate." While energy and enthusiasm can inspire some, it doesn't work for everyone. Even Rothman conceded, "Not everyone has a flame that can be lit."

Paths of Least Resistance

Many of the women I interviewed said the behaviors and beliefs that underlie their leadership style come naturally to them. I attribute this to two things: their socialization and the career paths they have chosen. Although socialization patterns and career paths are changing, the average age of the men and women who responded to the survey is 51—old enough to have had experiences that differed because of gender.

Until the 1960s, men and women received different signals about what was expected of them. To summarize a subject that many experts have explored in depth, women have been expected to be wives, mothers, community volunteers, teachers, and nurses. In all these roles, they are supposed to be cooperative, supportive, understanding, gentle, and to provide service to others. They are to derive satisfaction and a sense of self-esteem from helping others, including their spouses. While men have had to appear to be competitive, strong, tough, decisive, and in control, women have been allowed to be cooperative, emotional, supportive, and vulnerable. This may explain why women today are more likely than men to be interactive leaders.

Men and women have also had different career opportunities. Women were not expected to have careers, or at least not the same kinds of careers as men, so they either pursued different jobs or were simply denied opportunities men had. Women's career tracks have usually not included long series of organizational positions with formal authority and control of resources. Many women had their first work experiences outside the home as volunteers. While some of the challenges they faced as managers in volunteer organizations are the same as those in any business, in many ways, leading volunteers is different because of the absence of concrete rewards like pay and promotion.

As women entered the business world, they tended to find themselves in positions consistent with the roles they played at home: in staff positions rather than in line positions, supporting the work of others, and in functions like communications or human resources where they had relatively small budgets and few people reporting directly to them.

The fact that most women have lacked formal authority over others and control over resources means that by default they have had to find other ways to accomplish their work. As it turns out, the behaviors that were natural and/or socially acceptable for them have been highly successful in at least some managerial settings.

What came easily to women turned out to be a survival tactic. Although leaders often begin their careers doing what comes naturally and what fits within the constraints of the job, they also develop their skills and styles over time. The women's use of interactive leadership has its roots in socialization, and the women interviewees firmly believe that it benefits their organizations. Through the course of their careers, they have gained conviction that their style is effective. In fact, for some, it was their own success that caused them to formulate their philosophies about what motivates people, how to make good decisions, and what it takes to maximize business performance.

They now have formal authority and control over vast resources, but still they see sharing power and information as an asset rather than a liability. They believe that although pay and promotion are necessary tools of management, what people really want is to feel that they are contributing to a higher purpose and that they have the opportunity as individuals to learn and grow. The women believe that employees and peers perform better when they feel they are part of an organization and can share in its success. Allowing them to get involved and to work to their potential is a way of maximizing their contributions and using human resources most efficiently.

Another Kind of Diversity

The IWF survey shows that a nontraditional leadership style can be effective in organizations that accept it. This lesson comes especially hard to those who think of the corporate world as a game of survival of the fittest, where the fittest is always the strongest, toughest, most decisive, and powerful. Such a workplace seems to favor leaders who control people by controlling resources, and by controlling people, gain control of more resources. Asking for information and sharing decision-making power can be seen as serious disadvantages, but what is a disadvantage under one set of circumstances is an advantage under another. The "best" leadership style depends on the organizational context.

Only one of the women interviewees is in a traditional, large-scale company. More typically, the women's organizations are medium-sized and tend to have experienced fast growth and fast change. They demand performance and/or have a high proportion of professional workers. These organizations seem to create opportunities for women and are hospitable to those who use a nontraditional management style.

The degree of growth or change in an organization is an important factor in creating opportunities for women. When change is rampant, everything is up for grabs, and crises are frequent. Crises are generally not desirable, but they do create opportunities for people to prove themselves. Many of the women interviewees said they got their first break because their organizations were in turmoil.

Fast-changing environments also play havoc with tradition. Coming up through the ranks and being part of an established network is no longer important. What is important is how you perform. Also, managers in such environments are open to new solutions, new structures, and new ways of leading.

The fact that many of the women respondents are in organizations that have clear performance standards suggests that they have gained credibility and legitimacy by achieving results. In investment banking, venture capital, accounting, and executive placement, for instance, individual performance is easy to measure.

A high proportion of young professional workers—increasingly typical of organizations—is also a factor in some women's success. Young, educated professionals impose special requirements on their organizations. They demand to participate and contribute. In some cases, they have knowledge or talents their bosses don't have. If they are good performers, they have many employment options. It is easy to imagine that these professionals will respond to leaders who are inclusive and open, who enhance the self-worth of others, and who create a fun work environment. Interactive leaders are likely to win the co operation needed to achieve their goals.

Interactive leadership has proved to be effective, perhaps even advantageous, in organizations in which the women I interviewed have succeeded. As the work force increasingly demands participation and the economic environment increasingly requires rapid change, interactive leadership may emerge as the management style of choice for many organizations. For interactive leadership to take root more broadly, however, organizations must be willing to question the notion that the traditional command-and-control leadership style that has brought success in earlier decades is the only way to get results. This may be hard in some organizations, especially those with long histories of male-oriented, command-and-control leadership. Changing these organizations will not be easy. The fact that women are more likely than men to be interactive leaders raises the risk that these companies will perceive interactive leadership as "feminine" and automatically resist it.

Linking interactive leadership directly to being female is a mistake. We know that women are capable of making their way through corporations by adhering to the traditional corporate model and that they can wield power in ways similar to men. Indeed, some women may prefer that style. We also know from the survey findings that some men use the transformational leadership style.

Large, established organizations should expand their definition of effective leadership. If they were to do that, several things might happen, including the disappearance of the glass ceiling and the creation of a wider path for all sorts of executives—men and women—to attain positions of leadership. Widening the path will free potential leaders to lead in ways that play to their individual strengths. Then the newly recognized interactive leadership style can be valued and rewarded as highly as the command-and-control style has been for decades. By valuing a diversity of leadership styles, organizations will find the strength and flexibility to survive in a highly competitive, increasingly diverse economic environment.

Notes

1. Transactional and transformational leadership were first conceptualized by James McGregor Burns in *Leadership* (New York: Harper & Row, 1978) and later by Bernard Bass in *Leadership and Performance Beyond Expectations* (New York: Free Press, 1985).

The IWF Survey of Men and Women Leaders

THE INTERNATIONAL WOMEN'S FORUM was founded in 1982 to give prominent women leaders in diverse professions around the world a way to share their knowledge with each other and with their communities and countries. The organization now has some 37 forums in North America, Europe, Asia, Latin America, and the Middle East. To help other women advance and to educate the public about the contributions women can and are making in government, business, and other fields, the IWF created the Leadership Foundation. The Foundation commissioned me to perform the study of men and women leaders on which this article is based. I conducted the study with the help of Daniel McAllister and Gregory Stephens (Ph.D. students at the Graduate School of Management at the University of California, Irvine) in the spring of 1989.

The survey consisted of an eight-page questionnaire sent to all the IWF members. Each respondent was asked to supply the name of a man in a similar organization with similar responsibilities. The men received the same questionnaire as the IWF members. The respondents were similar in age, occupation, and educational level, which suggests that the matching effort was successful. The response rate was 31%.

The respondents were asked questions about their leadership styles, their organizations, work-family issues, and personal characteristics. The following are among the more intriguing findings, some of which contradict data reported in academic journals and the popular press:

- The women earn the same amount of money as their male counterparts. The average yearly income for men is $136,510; for women it is $140,573. (Most other studies have shown a wage gap between men and women.)

- The men's household income (their own and their spouse's) is much lower than that of the women— $166,454 versus $300,892. (Only 39% of the men have full-time employed spouses, as opposed to 71% of the women.)

- Both men and women leaders pay their female subordinates roughly $12,000 less than their male subordinates with similar positions and titles.

- Women are more likely than men to use transformational leadership—motivating others by transforming their self-interest into the goals of the organization.

- Women are much more likely than men to use power based on charisma, work record, and contacts (personal power) as opposed to power based on organizational position, title, and the ability to reward and punish (structural power).

- Most men and women describe themselves as having an equal mix of traits that are considered "feminine" (being excitable, gentle, emotional, submissive, sentimental, understanding, compassionate, sensitive, dependent), "masculine" (dominant, aggressive, tough, assertive, autocratic, analytical, competitive, independent), and "gender-neutral" (adaptive, tactful, sincere, conscientious, conventional, reliable, predictable, systematic, efficient).

- Women who do describe themselves as predominately "feminine" or "gender-neutral" report a higher level of followership among their female subordinates than women who describe themselves as "masculine."

- Approximately 67% of the women respondents are married. (Other studies report that only 40% to 50% of women executives are married.)

- Both married men and married women experience moderate levels of conflict between work and family domains. When there are children at home, women experience only slightly higher levels of conflict than men, even though they shoulder a much greater proportion of the child care—61% of the care versus 25% for the men.

Originally published in November–December 1990
Reprint 90608

About the Contributors

PETER CAPPELLI is the George W. Taylor Professor of Management and the director of the Center for Human Resources at the University of Pennsylvania's Wharton School in Philadelphia.

PERRY CHRISTENSEN, the former director of human resource strategy and planning at Merck & Company, is now with WFD Consulting in Boston, Massachusetts.

JESSICA DEGROOT is founder and executive director of the Third Path, a nonprofit agency based in Philadelphia focused on the integration of work and personal life.

ROBIN J. ELY is an associate professor at Harvard Business School.

JOYCE K. FLETCHER is a professor of management at the Center for Gender in Organizations at Simmons Graduate School of Management and a senior research scholar at the Jean Baker Miller Training Institute at the Wellesley College Centers for Women in Wellesley, Massachusetts.

STEWART D. FRIEDMAN is director of the Leadership Program and the Work/Life Integration Project at the University of Pennsylvania's Wharton School in Philadelphia.

MONIKA HAMORI is an assistant professor of human resources management at Instituto de Empresa in Madrid, Spain.

SYLVIA ANN HEWLETT is the founder and president of the Center for Work-Life Policy, a New York–based not-for-profit organization. She also heads up the Gender and Public Policy Program at the School of International and Public Affairs at Columbia University in New York.

CAROLYN BUCK LUCE is the global managing partner for Ernst & Young's heath sciences industry practice in New York. She is the cochair for the Center for Work-Life Policy's Hidden Brain Drain task force.

DOUGLAS M. MCCRACKEN is the CEO of Deloitte Consulting, a global business of Deloitte Touche Tohmatsu. He is also chairman of Deloitte & Touche LLP in the United States.

DEBRA E. MEYERSON is a professor of management at the Center for Gender in Organizations at the Simmons Graduate School of Management in Boston and a visiting professor at Stanford University's Graduate School of Business in Palo Alto, California.

JUDY B. ROSENER is a faculty member at the Graduate School of Management at the University of California, Irvine.

FELICE N. SCHWARTZ is president and founder of Catalyst, a national not-for-profit research and advisory organization that works with business to effect change for women.

DAVID A. THOMAS is a professor at Harvard Business School.

Index